LUTHER
and the
HUNGRY POOR

LUTHER
and the
HUNGRY POOR

Gathered Fragments

Samuel Torvend

Fortress Press
Minneapolis

LUTHER AND THE HUNGRY POOR
Gathered Fragments

Cover image: Woodcut from Martin Luther's *Kirchen Postilla* (Wittenberg: Hans Lufft, 1562). Artist unknown. Courtesy of the Richard C. Kessler Reformation Collection, Pitts Theology Library, Candler School of Theology, Emory University.

The following interior images are courtesy of the Richard C. Kessler Reformation Collection, Pitts Theology Library, Candler School of Theology, Emory University: 1.1, 1.2, 1.3, 1.4, 2.1, 2.2, 2.3, 2.4, 3.2, 3.3, 3.4, 3.5, 3.6, 4.1, 4.2, 4.3, 4.4, 5.2, 5.3, 5.4, 5.5, 5.6, 6.1, 6.2, 6.3, 6.4, 6.6, 7.2, 7.3, 7.4, 7.5.

Cover design: Laurie Ingram
Book design: James Korsmo

Library of Congress Cataloging-in-Publication Data
Torvend, Samuel.
Luther and the hungry poor : gathered fragments / Samuel Torvend.
  p. cm.
Includes bibliographical references and index.
ISBN 978-0-8006-6238-7 (alk. paper)
  1. Luther, Martin, 1483-1546. 2. Economics—Religious aspects—Christianity.
  3. Poverty—Religious aspects—Christianity. 4. Hunger—Religious
aspects—Christianity. I. Title.
BR333.5.E2T67 2008
261.8'325‹dc22

                                               2007043167

11   10   09   08   1   2   3   4   5   6   7   8   9   10

To my father and mother
E. Silas and Alice Kjesbu Torvend

*"Wisdom is better than jewels, and all that you may desire
cannot compare with her."*
Proverbs 8:11

CONTENTS

Contents

PREFACE

I write these words in my home, close to the Puget Sound, surrounded by towering fir and oak trees, with a glimpse of Mount Rainier in the far distance. I am not the first in my family to live here. When my grandparents came to this region at the beginning of the twentieth century, they were part of that great wave of immigrants who moved to the western reaches of the continent in search of economic security, to a region marked by the abundant gifts of forest, field, and sea. Hard work and fertile soil allowed my grandparents and parents to enjoy the fruit of their labor. They prospered. They never lacked food and drink.

Over the past thirty years, new immigrants have contributed to the astonishing economic growth of the region. Computer technology has joined aircraft building, financial investment, transpacific trade, and medical research to create levels of wealth unimagined in the late 1960s. House building continues unabated as Asians, Pacific Islanders, and Central Americans arrive in search of their fortunes. Yet in the midst of growing wealth and its ostentatious display by the new bourgeoisie, the region is also marked by some of the highest levels of food insecurity and child malnourishment in the nation. While many Americans might associate hunger with "impoverished" Southern states, the line of hunger growth has actually shifted westward and now runs from Washington and Oregon to the Southwest and Texas. The surprising fact is that the vast majority of the hungry poor in the Pacific Northwest are children of parents who work one or two jobs at minimum wage, widows living on minuscule pensions, military dependents, and the mentally ill who have been discharged from state institutions because of cuts in governmental funding. Set alongside the very public wealth of the region is the growing incidence of food insecurity, a reality that appears only infrequently in the media and, consequently, in the consciousness of the regional population.

How can manifest wealth among the few coexist with the impoverishment of the increasing many? One would think that in a nation boastful of its financial resources and marked by a vast network of charitable giving the growth of poverty and hunger would prove odious and lead political and social leaders to work steadfastly for the elimination of a condition many associate with underdeveloped nations. Such misery set next to much affluence has led me, as a professor of the history of Christianity, to ask if there are voices in the Christian tradition that have considered the most basic human necessities: food and drink. Thus, this book on early Lutheran responses to the hungry poor is one attempt to bring to the fore a significant voice in the history of Christianity.

While many popular works on church history portray Martin Luther as a reformer concerned primarily with correcting church abuses and extolling the primacy of the Bible, grace, faith, freedom, and doctrine, he was also thrust into and wrote on the economic, political, and social questions and crises of his day. He was vividly aware of an emerging global economy, the growth of poverty, the stark reality of hunger, and the failure of government and religious charities to address the fundamental need for food and drink.

Perhaps Luther's most systematic work is the German or Large Catechism he published in 1529. In his explanation of the first article of the Apostles' Creed, he speaks briefly and beautifully of the various means through which humans receive physical nourishment. However, no systematic work can be found that contains a theological or social ethic focused on food and hunger. One must look here and there, discovering fragments that can be pieced together: a sermon, a letter, a preface, biblical commentaries, treatises, theological or sacramental works. In the various fragments of Luther's writings, one can discern early in his career a linking of theology and ethics, sacraments and social welfare.

Luther was engaged in a project to reform church and society, not one or the other, not theology or social ethics but both. The reform he advanced, however, was not the first in the history of Christianity. The reader will note that the first chapter of this book, a prelude as it were, sets forth the claim that Jesus of Nazareth, the central figure in Christianity, was committed to reform, a theological reform focused on real human need. From this prelude, the discussion proceeds in fairly chronological order beginning with Luther's printing of his Ninety-five

Theses in 1517 and ending with the publication of his preface to the Leisnig Fraternal Agreement of 1523, the first major "Lutheran" congregational and civic response to the hungry poor.

A theological assertion in the order is presented here: Luther's questions about the spiritual economy of late medieval Christianity are set next to the incidence of hunger and poverty in early sixteenth-century Germany; justification by grace is set next to the human and suffering Christ; and his criticism of a hierarchically structured church is set next to a baptismal community at work in the world—the life of the risen Christ, so he believed, at work in the contours of daily life. Thus, the social dimension of a theological claim is revealed in these pairings. At the same time, justification, Christ, baptism, faith, and service form the foundation of a social ethic. They lead forward to Luther's discussion of hunger in the Scriptures and his wedding of sacrament and social welfare.

But, then, it would appear that another piecing together of fragments is present in the order of this book. Luther used the teaching on justification by grace in his reform of the Mass, the central and public act of the Christian community. The reformed Mass itself was intended to reveal and teach the presence of Christ coming to the worshipping assembly with mercy in the midst of human misery. One would enter this assembly but once through the washing of baptism and, according to Luther, be immersed repeatedly in the proclamation and interpretation of the Word of God and the celebration of the Lord's Supper. Why the word and sacraments, a "theological" reality? So that the Christian assembly might come to know and enact its purpose in the world, a social reality.

And there is this: the possibility that Christians and Christian communities would utterly fail in what they had been formed to be through the word and the sacraments. While Luther spoke clearly and forcefully concerning Christian and civic responses to the hungry poor, he frequently acknowledged the easy assimilation of Christians and their leaders to cultural practices and convictions at odds with what he considered the gospel of Jesus Christ. Great hope and great dismay could not be separated.

In this book, then, one can find texts published early in Luther's career that, perhaps unknown to him, set forth the beginning or fragmentary foundation of a social ethic focused on the hungry poor. His social ethic emerged out of his study and preaching of the word of God and the celebration of the sacraments. And it was lived out persuasively and lovingly by Christians who were part and parcel of the economic, political, and social fabric of a cultural epoch: Germany in the early sixteenth century. We do well, then, to recognize Luther in his own culture and time rather than our own. We do well to resist the temptation to translate uncritically his thought and projects into the present moment. He could not have imagined, for instance, the constitutional separation of church and state, religious pluralism, or ecumenical alliances around pressing social questions. Were he to appear from the distant past and view our affluence, technology, and inequities, perhaps he would simply stutter. Perhaps he would cluck with surprised appreciation at the vast network of religious communities that carry on today the heroic work among the hungry poor begun, albeit haltingly, in 1523. Perhaps he would groan with dismay that government has increasingly abdicated what he considered its singular responsibility: to care for the most vulnerable in society, a service for the common good. We do not know. We have only hints.

This work grew out of courses and conversations with Frank Henderson; the late Christopher Kiesling, o.p.; Gordon Lathrop; the late Michael Marx, o.s.b.; and Gail Ramshaw. The project has been aided by continued conversation with my students who have taken my courses on Liturgy and Social Justice, Luther, Lutheran Christianity, Christian Theology of Food and Hunger, and Sacramental Theology at the St. Paul Seminary School of Divinity (University of St. Thomas, St. Paul, Minnesota), Aquinas Institute of Theology (St. Louis, Missouri), Saint Mary's University (Winona, Minnesota), Seattle University (Seattle, Washington), and Pacific Lutheran University (Tacoma, Washington). I have been inspired and challenged by the pioneering work of the late Virgil Michael, o.s.b., monk of St. John's Abbey, and Carter Lindberg, Professor of Church History Emeritus at Boston University.

I am especially indebted to Don and Naomi Nothstein, who provided funding for faculty-student research in memory of Naomi's father, Kelmer Roe, professor of Greek and religion at Pacific Lutheran University. I was ably assisted and enlightened by the work of Matthew Tabor, the first Kelmer Roe student scholar. The reception of the Edgar and Margaret Schick Fellowship in Religion and Public Life from the

Luther Institute (Washington, D.C.) and a Regency Advancement Award from Pacific Lutheran University enabled me to do research in Germany and complete the writing of this work during a sabbatical. Douglas Oakman, Dean of the Division of Humanities, and Patricia Killen, University Provost at PLU, offered great support in the completion of this project. I am grateful to Michael West, Marshall Johnson, Josh Messner, and James Korsmo—all of Fortress Press—for their wise advice and care of this book.

My parents, Silas Torvend and Alice Kjesbu Torvend, planted the seeds of this project many years ago by welcoming many guests to our family table. Frank, Rex, and Rebecca Rainsberger continue that hospitality at table so central to the Christian life. Andrew Stone and Stephen Crippen bind together the sharing of food and drink in the Mass, at their dining room table, and among the hungry poor. To these family members and friends, I offer my thanks.

I

Baskets Filled with Fragments

Eating and Drinking in the Presence of Jesus

Let us begin with two meals: one held for the wealthy few in a king's palace, the other for the many poor in an open field. In one the powerful gather to feast; in the other the powerless look for food and drink. Two meals, two worlds, history viewed from "above" and from "below."

Serving Death or Life

On the occasion of his birthday, Herod Antipas, ruler of Galilee and son of Herod the Great, hosted a great banquet (Mark 6:14-29). The elite of the region—courtiers, army officers of the occupation force, and high-ranking officials—were invited to dine at table with the Roman-appointed tetrarch. Mark writes that in the course of the meal, Herod became so enchanted with the dancing of his new wife's daughter that when he promised her she could have anything she wanted, he was surprised to hear her say, "The head of John the baptizer." Because he had criticized the marriage of Herod to Herodias, saying, "It is not lawful for you to have your brother's wife," John had been arrested and was now imprisoned. At Herod's command a guard was dispatched from the banquet room to the prison, John was beheaded, and his severed head was carried into the banquet on a platter. The daughter offered the head to her mother in the presence of the guests, a gruesome gift and a terrifying reminder that criticism of the ruler or his wife would be met with reprisal. At the center of a banquet intended to celebrate life, death itself was served up on a royal plate, the voice of a prophet silenced.

Mark sets alongside this narration of a festive meal marked by seduction and revenge the story of a great crowd following Jesus into a deserted place (Mark 6:30-44).[1] Such an occurrence was not unknown to the Jews of Palestine; after all, their ancestors had followed Moses into the wilderness of Sinai on their journey to the Promised Land.[2] Upon seeing the crowd, writes Mark, Jesus had compassion for them because they were like "sheep without

Figure 1.1. Lucas Cranach the Elder, *Death of John the Baptist*, 1531, from the title page of Luther's "Commentary on the Alleged Imperial Edict," 1531.

a shepherd" (6:34). The use of the phrase "sheep without a shepherd" repeats a common image employed by the Hebrew prophets who criticized rulers—shepherds—who oppressed their people and "fleeced" them of their produce or wages.[3] At the same time the use of "shepherd" invokes the memory of God as Israel's faithful shepherd,[4] the one who guided the people out of Egyptian slavery into the wilderness, the one to whom Israel had recourse later in their history when their human "shepherds" failed to rule the people with justice and mercy.

Mark then notes that as the day lengthened, the disciples came to Jesus and asked him to send the people away so that they could "go into the surrounding country and villages and buy something for themselves to eat" (6:36). Rejecting their advice—for what impoverished peasant had money to buy food?—Jesus ordered the disciples to give the people something to eat. Finding only five loaves and two fish, Jesus had the people sit down, blessed God for the bread and fish he had taken in his hands, and then gave them to the disciples for distribution among the people. The account concludes on a remarkable note: the two fish and the five loaves were sufficient to feed more than five thousand people.[5]

In contrast to the lethal banquet held in a royal palace, hungry people were fed in a deserted place with twelve baskets of bread fragments left over. With Herod the ruler, death was served at the meal; with Jesus the prophet, the promise of life.

Christians have long seen in the actions of Jesus the gestures that accompany the Eucharist: taking bread, blessing God, and breaking and distributing the fragments. Indeed, Mark's story of this wilderness feeding might actually reflect the meal custom practiced among the Christians to whom he was writing his gospel in the 60s.[6] That is, the story could hold two very

Figure 1.2. *Feeding the 5000*, 1540, from one of Luther's commentaries on the epistles and gospels appointed for Advent.

different references at the same time: a *memory* of the meal practice of the historical Jesus and an *invitation* for early Christians to recognize in their own meal practice the feeding of Hebrew slaves in the desert and Jesus' bread and fish supper with a great crowd. God provides food, unexpectedly, for poor slaves in the wilderness; Jesus blesses God for bread and fish, two staples in the diet of poor Mediterranean peasants; early Christians share bread, fish, and wine as they gather in the name and memory of the Crucified One.

God the Patron Meeting Real Human Need

New Testament scholars who employ the tools of social scientific research have deepened and expanded our understanding of the economic, social, and political context in which Jesus kept meals. Their work asks us to consider first-century Roman Palestine, a colony occupied by a foreign military force, in which an impoverished peasant population paid tithes to the priestly elites who administered the temple. Many of these priests came from established and wealthy families, some of whom were eager to cooperate with the Romans. Such collaboration could be interpreted as a realistic response to overwhelming military force: it was better to maintain peace and order than encourage or engage in resistance when it was clear that any rebellion would be swiftly crushed, the hills of Palestine filled with crucifixions.[7] Scholars of the political economy alive in Roman Palestine during the first century suggest that cooperation benefited those who were able to cooperate: Roman "patrons" could distribute what they considered "their land" to select and wealthy Judean "clients."[8] Such clients could then amass vast agricultural estates. The small landholdings of the poor who could not compete with the great estates or could not pay the various taxes required of them were gobbled up, as it were, producing more landless workers and a growing population of the poor. In addition to a temple tax, colonized Jews were forced to pay a tax to the Roman emperor, a human who claimed to be a god, a "god" whose reign was marked by the occupation and confiscation of land, the imposition of Roman cultural and religious values, utter disregard for the hungry poor, a brutal death for anyone who questioned Roman "order," and the practice of religiously political rituals that supported and thus sanctioned such an order.

In this context we find two biblical memories and two images of God colliding. The first memory, found in the Hebrew Bible, corresponded with many of the realities alive in first-century Palestine: the experience of a monarchical and stratified social life focused on Jerusalem and the temple, where healthy, observant, "pure" Jewish males and their families offered tithes to priests who controlled and communicated the image of a "pure" and holy God.[9] In Jerusalem, "holy Zion," contracts were negotiated and signed that distributed rich agricultural land to wealthy elites. As Jesus notes Jerusalem widows, having lost their houses in order to pay the required tithe, were rendered homeless and hungry (Mark 12:38-40). Beware of those who pray loudly and seek the best seats at banquets, he cautions; they devour widows' houses. To this hilltop city the Roman governor would send his army to ensure peace and order whenever pilgrims arrived to celebrate the ancient feast of their liberation from another deified ruler. Indeed, the religious reforms promoted by the Pharisees can be seen as the genuine desire to extend the holiness of God into all aspects of life, a spiritual form of resistance to the presence of Rome's many gods. Israel's renewers who demanded holiness were also keen on drawing sharp distinctions between the "pure" and the "impure"—between the observant and the righteous, the "insiders" who were considered close to God, and the nonobservant and socially marginalized who were considered "outside" the presence of a "holy" God. These included the chronically sick or mentally ill, menstruating or hemorrhaging women, impoverished peasants, prostitutes, tax collectors, and Gentiles—the many who could not fulfill the laws of holiness, the many who believed they were "sinners," socially and religiously marginalized.[10]

There was a second biblical memory, scholars suggest, one vitally alive among the peasants of Jesus' home, the Galilee. It was the ancient memory of the exodus from bitter slavery, of God caring for and leading a sometimes mutinous and ill-formed community into the desert where rocks gushed forth fresh water, and manna and quail appeared at dawn and dusk. It was the memory of life in a decentralized community, guided by judges and prophets, a confederation of tribes that worshipped the Deliverer and the Provider. It was the memory of the promise that there would be sufficient milk and honey for

Figure 1.3. *First Passover observed,* 1670, from a later edition of Luther's Complete or German Bible, 1534.

all, not just the few, so that the people might live robustly in the land. It was a memory invoked every year in the celebration of Passover as the people ate and drank the story of deliverance from the "house of bondage."

Jesus, it would seem, was influenced by this second memory, this "theology" that he announced in word and embodied in deed, his "social practice," a criticism of and an alternative to the first and "normative" memory.[11] In contrast to the oppressive reign of Caesar the imperial patron, what Jesus called the religious "banditry" of first-century temple practice (Mark 11:12-25),[12] and the image of a "holy" God who ostensibly favored the "pure" and the "righteous," Israel's divine patron, the Deliverer and Provider, desired to meet real human need. In the coming reign of this God, the hungry will "receive" daily bread and be free to glean on the Sabbath to ensure that their families can eat (Mark 2:23-28). The onerous weight of debts will be forgiven, an invocation of the Jubilee and Sabbatical promises (Lev. 25:8-55; Deut. 15:1-6). Widows will live secure in their homes, freed from a burdensome tax and delivered from the evil of homelessness and hunger (Mark 12:38-44).

Jesus' commitment to the coming of God's reign envisioned a time when the temple and its ritual practices would manifest God's gracious patronage for the many as practiced in the Passover ritual: a "social practice" rooted in a "theology" in which the people, even the hungry "outsider," would share sufficient food and drink (Exod. 12:43-49). Where the Deliverer and Provider is worshipped, there is blessing and life "for many," not only for the Jew but for the many nations of the earth, a reinsertion of the ancient Israelite hope that all people, including "impure" foreigners and eunuchs of ambiguous sexuality, would enjoy communion with God on the holy mountain.[13] Thus, Jesus' open table fellowship (Mark 2:13-17) and his feeding the hungry poor (Mark 6:30-44; 8:1-9) can be seen as prophetic signs that embodied his commitment to the coming reign of Israel's gracious patron. Yet to accept and advance this "memory," one that would inevitably clash with the theology and social practice of the first, would be to follow in the "narrow way," the way that eventually led to Jerusalem, conflict, betrayal, and death.[14]

Faithful and Failed Meal Practices

It should come as no surprise, then, that scholars of Christian origins suggest that groups of early Christians kept a meal practice that may have looked like a potluck—a "common share meal," perhaps an agape meal—in which each one offered what he or she could and received according to need, an echo of the feeding of the five thousand, a domestic enactment of the "open" feast on God's holy mountain.[15] Indeed, the Acts of the Apostles sets the "breaking of the bread" next to the reality or at least the potent dream of having all things in common, of selling possessions and distributing the proceeds to those in need (2:43-47), the equitable sharing of bread extended into and shaping a larger sharing of resources across distinctions of gender, race, ethnic heritage, age, health, and class. It would seem that Jesus' practice of "open commen-sality," of sharing food and drink across invisible but real economic, religious, social, and political borders, flowed into the practice of the early Christians. Yet the New Testament makes clear that the followers of Jesus could fail.

Paul sarcastically rebukes the Christians at Corinth for their fac-tions, the socioeconomic divisions manifested in their keeping of the meal (1 Cor. 11:17-34). There is no "Lord's Supper," because some have sufficient food and drink while others go hungry. At least some of the Corinthian Christians seem incapable of "discerning the body," that is, the Lord's body, the Christian community itself, which is intended to transcend the social division and economic stratification found everywhere in the larger society. James accuses some in the Christian assembly of giving seats of honor to the wealthy while the poor are told to stand or sit, a posture of social servitude or shame (James 2:1-13). "Do you with your acts of favoritism really believe in our glori-ous Lord Jesus Christ?" asks the author of the letter. We read of those who participate in "love-feasts," perhaps a common shared meal, in which ungodly intruders distort the feast by feeding only themselves (Jude 12). As one ancient manuscript notes, "They are shepherds who care only for themselves." Such persons "deny our only Master and Lord, Jesus Christ" (v. 4). There are those who "revel in their dissipa-tion while they feast with you," notes the second letter of Peter, their "hearts trained in greed," an allusion to the relationship between greed and economic exclusivity (2:13-14). They deny the Master by their avarice (2:1-3). What they confess with their lips is contradicted by their social practice.

Such texts set forth the sad prospect of a closed meal for the few, the failure to share food and drink equitably in the community, or the power of greed as economic hunger and gluttonous act. The pos-sibility of contradicting the meal practice of Jesus and the "theology" it implied, of transforming the Christian meal into a social practice for the elite or the "pure," was ever-present as Christian communities emerged in urban settings around the Mediterranean Sea and beyond. Closed or exclusive meals and the denigration of the hungry poor, so remarkably alive in the larger culture, had been critiqued by Jesus who ate and drank with outcasts, who welcomed women at table, who offered bread and fish to hungry peasants. Yet as Paul, Peter, James, and

Jude suggest, the memory of Jesus' surprising practice, rooted in his theology of God, the Deliverer and Provider, could be overwhelmed by the normative practice of the ancient world: the elite few have much to eat and drink; the many poor scrape and search for bread and fish.

Prophetic Reform

What these accounts of faithful and failed meal practices suggest is not only the struggle to share food and drink in diverse cultural contexts but also the awareness that what *is* practiced can stand in contrast to what *ought to be* practiced, each expressing a theology and a worldview. An originating vision can be clouded or obscured by other or later competing practices and visions. Thus, we find Jesus frequently criticized for one of the central characteristics of his public life: sharing food and drink, as guest or host, with social outcasts and poor, hungry people—a critique of existing meal practice (that is, "pure" insiders do not eat with the "impure" outsiders) and a reforming of that practice in light of his theological vision (that is, "All ate and were filled," Mark 6:42).

Mark's narration of the feeding of five thousand from a few loaves of bread and two fish was intended to invoke the image of the prophet Elisha, who took a limited amount of barley and, surprisingly, fed one hundred people (2 Kings 4:42-44). Perhaps Christians have not usually referred to Jesus as a prophet or prophetic reformer; Messiah (Matt. 1:1), Savior (Luke 2:11), and Word of God (John 1:1-3) are among the metaphors that have enjoyed considerable popularity in the tradition. Yet

Figure 1.4. Lucas Cranach, *Christ's demonstration in the Temple*, 1521, from the "Passional Christi und Antichristi."

Jesus saw his public life within that prophetic tradition: in the Gospels he tells the disciples of John the Baptist, albeit obliquely, that he is a prophet (Matt. 11:2-6), claims the words of the prophet Isaiah as his public mission (Luke 4:14-19), and likens himself to the prophet Elijah (Luke 4:21-30).[16] As a prophetic witness to the reign of God, the Deliverer and Provider, the gracious patron of all, Jesus called people to *metanoia*, to a changed understanding and practice, to reform (Mark 1:15).

In contrast to a deeply popular view of Jesus as the revelation of something previously unheard of and thus entirely new, a closer and contextual reading of the New Testament suggests that the historical Jesus understood himself and was perceived as a prophetic reformer. He did not abolish the central human social and religious act of keeping a meal, of sharing food and drink; as a first-century Palestinian Jew, it would have been impossible for him to do so. Rather, this essential human activity, interpreted through the experience and texts of Israel, was re-formed, shaped anew, as a central embodiment of his theological vision, a vision rooted in and shaped by the celebration of Passover and its theology of God, the liberator and sustainer of life.

Why would such a ritual celebration be perceived as a source of reform? As a pilgrimage feast Passover was a communal celebration, available to all, that brought hope to ordinary people who lived in poverty under an oppressive regime governed by a man who claimed to be a god.[17] The keeping of this meal, the sharing of food and drink among the family and even with the stranger, the "impure" foreigner, envisioned the profound nearness of a benevolent and merciful God to the many, not just the few. Under the looming power of the Roman *imperium*, the celebration of Passover could express the hope for a merciful and gracious patron who responded to real human need. Indeed, Jesus' instruction to pray for daily bread was not intended as a divine sanction for food already possessed; it was an earnest plea for food not yet present (Luke 11:3). It was also this: a confession of trust in the one who promised "a feast of rich food, of well-aged wines" for all people (Isa. 25:6). Between the plea and the promise, there was a space in which the call for reform was heard and enacted. As the tragic end of Jesus' life made clear, it was a dangerous place in which to dwell.

This is to suggest that reform was not an invention of sixth-century Benedictines or eleventh-century Cistercians or thirteenth-century

Franciscans or sixteenth-century Lutherans. Instead, reform was at the very heart of Jesus' own public work and the various early Christian communities that emerged in the Mediterranean region during the course of the first century. It is to suggest that Jesus, the prophetic reformer, announced in word and sign the coming of God's gracious reign or patronage, a reign that would engage the economic, political, and social conditions in which first-century Palestinians lived. It is to suggest that his theology of God, the Deliverer and Provider, was expressed in a social practice, the two never separated into "spiritual" and "secular," a distinction that emerged, nonetheless, quickly and almost pervasively in the cultural and intellectual contexts in which the Christian movement took root. A person could live only one life, a unity, a whole—life in its many dimensions—in the presence of God. It is to suggest, as well, that Jesus of Nazareth was acutely aware of the hungry poor who populated the region in which he grew to adulthood and among whom he shared food and drink, bread and fish. His "open commensality" was a central and public characteristic, a prophetic sign, of the nearness of the reign of God.[18]

Twelve baskets were taken up, Mark notes, full of bread fragments, but to where they were taken, we do not know. One may speculate that they were carried into the many Christian communities that sprang forth around and beyond the Mediterranean Sea, signs of God's patronage among the hungry poor now identified and received as the body of Christ, the bread of life, the new manna for this world's hunger.

In the New Testament, that collection of gospels and letters so beloved by the sixteenth-century reformers, there is no systematic theology of kingdom, prophet, or meal. There are only fragments: parables, sayings, invitations, menus, and vignettes. There are only allusions to the practice of gathering for a meal and extending that meal into the wider culture. Yet the fragments and allusions were enough—enough to establish a pattern of sending forth food and drink from the Christian supper to the hungry poor. In that return to the spring of early Christian practice so ardently promoted by the sixteenth-century reformers, fragments and allusions were enough to continue the work of reform in another cultural epoch among that "great crowd without anything to eat" (Mark 8:1).

PART ONE

Foundations

2
THE CHURCH FISHES FOR WEALTH

Early Awareness of the Hungry Poor

To say the least, there was not one reformation during the sixteenth century but various reformations. The diversity of these reforming movements—from Anabaptist to Zwinglian—reflected the temperaments, training, and interests of those who called for the reform of church and society. Thus, Roman Catholic reform focused on clerical education and church administration. The Calvinist project was attentive to the reform of worship and ethics. Martin Luther, on the other hand, emerged as a reformer who began and held his "evangelical" reform within theology.[1] Indeed, various contemporary biographies of Luther[2] narrate the existential anxiety that plagued the monk, priest, and professor until his scholarly research and incessant questioning yielded what he experienced as a theological breakthrough in his understanding of the relationship between God and humanity.

That dogged questioning, influenced by late medieval nominalism, Luther's *Anfechtung*, and his diligent study of the biblical text, led to his initial foray into public life. In October 1517 he extended an invitation to the University of Wittenberg faculty to discuss and debate ninety-five theological claims. The public posting of theses was nothing unusual in the academic life of a Renaissance university. Rather, it was the ordinary means through which faculty and students, who could not have dreamed of telephones or e-mail, would notify each other of a normal university practice: a debate or discussion concerning a topic or issue of current interest.

Theological Critique of Indulgence Sales

That Luther's posting of his Ninety-five Theses was sparked by his objection to the sale of indulgences has been frequently interpreted as a critique of a church-sanctioned practice, a practice that could grow easily in a religious atmosphere dominated by ambiguity concerning one's salvation. Indeed, the question asked by late medieval Christians focused intensely on how one might cooperate with the grace of Christ to receive a merciful judgment from God on the Last Day. Johannes Tetzel, the Dominican friar and indulgence preacher in Germany, was adept at answering that question in an urgent and appealing manner. He encouraged his listeners to care for themselves by purchasing indulgences that would diminish their time in purgatory, that postmortem condition or place in which they would be prepared for heaven: "Run, all of you, for the salvation of your souls. Be [as] quick and concerned about redemption as about the temporal goods you doggedly pursue from day till night."[3] He

Figure 2.1. Johann Vogel, *Johannes Tetzel and his indulgence chest,* a late 17th c. portrait of the German indulgence preacher.

also urged them, in heartrending language, to care for their beloved dead: "Do you not hear the voices of your dead parents and other people, screaming and saying: 'We are suffering severe punishments and pain [in purgatory], from which you could rescue us with a few alms, if only you would?' "[4] The people of Wittenberg, whose financial assets allowed them to purchase indulgences, flocked to the seller of these spiritual favors. It was on their return to Wittenberg that Luther, their priest and confessor, heard of this preaching. To say the least, he was appalled.[5]

To question the sale of indulgences was not, for Luther, simply a matter of placing this questionable practice under the intense light of Scripture, theology, and canon law, a light that would expose its inherent theological problems. The Ninety-five Theses demonstrate Luther's awareness that an indulgence paper and the coins used to buy it were only the tip of a much larger issue. In his theses Luther argued that God desires to forgive humans who are truly repentant, who manifest a genuine conversion of life, a turning toward God, the root meaning of the word *repentance*.[6] Theologically, Luther asserted that God's regard for human beings is marked by forgiveness, since to be forgiving is within God's nature. Would God forgive those who possessed an indulgence but demonstrated no genuine conversion of life, no "repentance"? Did the indulgence trade—an external practice—obscure something of far greater significance: the turning of the inner person toward God?

Luther argued that the church possessed only one "treasure," a treasure given by God through Christ: "Without want of consideration we say that the keys of the church, given by the merits of Christ, are that treasure."[7] For sixteenth-century Christians the "keys of the church" were understood as the power to forgive sin or to deny forgiveness. In the context of the late medieval quest for salvation—the urgent desire to share eternal life with God and with all the redeemed—the church's ability to forgive or not forgive sin was perceived and experienced by many if not most people as a remarkable power upon which one's eternal fate depended. That "power," what Luther preferred to call a "treasure," was traced to the words of Jesus addressed to Peter in the Gospel of Matthew: "I tell you, you are Peter [Greek *pétros*, 'rock'], and on this rock I will build my church, and the gates of Hades will not prevail against it. I will give you the keys of the kingdom of heaven, and whatever you bind on earth will be bound in heaven, and whatever you lose on earth will be loosed in heaven" (Matt. 16:18-19). The power to bind and loose had come to be interpreted in Western theology as the power to forgive or deny forgiveness, a power, so many believed, first given to Peter.

By the sixteenth century the capacity to forgive was understood as a sacramental power given by Peter to his successors, the bishops of Rome, and, through the sacrament of ordination, to the priests of the church.[8] By calling into question the church-sponsored sale of indulgences, Luther called into question the one who sanctioned the sale of spiritual favors, the pope, the bishop of Rome. Here the ecclesiological or church-related dimension of the criticism came into play, for Luther was questioning the wisdom of church leaders and the theology of ordained indulgence preachers, public ministers of the church. How could one trust the word of those who made something on the periphery—indulgences—a central matter in the quest for salvation? Indeed, if the pope actually has the power to forgive punishments due to sin, why not do so now and relieve all Christians of undue anxiety?

"The true treasure of the church," wrote Luther, "is the most holy gospel of the glory and grace of God."[9] This gospel and this grace, so Luther would argue, should be shared freely. Again, the theological claim comes to the fore: God is gracious and desires that spiritual "goods," forgiveness among them,

Figure 2.2. *Earliest portrait of Luther as a monk, 1519, from the cover page of a sermon preached by Luther in Leipzig on the Feast of Sts. Peter and Paul.*

be offered among the people of God without payment. "Any truly repentant Christian has a right to full remission of penalty and guilt [for sin], even without indulgence letters."[10] He continued his criticism of the practice by juxtaposing "gospel" next to "indulgence." "The treasures of the gospel are the nets with which one formerly fished for men of wealth. The treasures of indulgences are nets with which one now fishes for *the wealth of men.* The indulgences the demagogues acclaim as the greatest graces are actually understood to be such only insofar as they promote gain."[11] "It is certain," he wrote, "that when money clinks in the money chest, greed and avarice can be increased."[12]

The Hungry Poor in Germany

By linking what he considered the false "treasure" of indulgences with "greed and avarice" and linking the true "grace" of forgiveness with the "inestimable gift of God," Luther demonstrated that he was mindful of social realities as well as theological claims. Indeed, who could afford to buy what the indulgence preachers claimed was necessary for anyone who desired to enjoy the fullness of eternal life? Why only those who possessed sufficient monetary assets? Where one can actually purchase spiritual favors or goods, the wealthy benefit but the poor lose. This is to suggest that in the social context of sixteenth-century Germany, concern for one's eternal salvation was inextricably linked to one's social and economic status. The wealthy would have little trouble buying indulgences, purchasing masses for the dead, endowing churches, going on pilgrimages (and thus not working), contributing to charities, or commissioning religious artwork that would adorn worship spaces. What then would be the eternal fate of the working poor, the landless poor, the destitute, the homeless, and the chronically ill who would find it almost impossible to assist themselves or their dead relatives?

It goes without saying that scholarly attention to the social and economic realities at play in the initial stages of the Reformation has emerged rather recently. Yet given the difficulties of assessing that reality across the landscape of early modern Europe, many would suggest that "by the sixteenth century, poverty had become a more insistent presence in more people's lives and in more kinds of lives than ever before."[13] In their study of early modern poverty, for instance, Catharina Lis and Hugo Soly note that while it is difficult to

Figure 2.3. David Deuchar, *Death comes for a poor German child,* 1803, an etching based on the original 16th c. drawing by Hans Holbein.

gauge accurately the proportion of actual poor or marginally poor in sixteenth-century Germany, it would appear that at least 50 if not 65 percent of the population were living on the edge of subsistence, unsure each day as to where they would find an adequate supply of food to feed themselves and family members.[14] "As much as 25 per cent of the population was chronically underfed. . . . All these people were directly, starkly vulnerable to natural disasters and fluctuations in agrarian and commercial markets. All were perched precariously at the edge of poverty."[15] Is it possible that sizable portions of the German population were religiously disenfranchised simply because they were poor and could not contribute financially to their own spiritual destiny?

"Christians are to be taught," Luther wrote, "that [the one] who gives to the poor or lends to the needy does a better deed than [the one] who buys indulgences."[16] While Luther did not intend to offer an analysis of hunger or poverty in his Ninety-five Theses, he did allude to the social and economic plight of his fellow Germans by making reference to the manner in which indulgence purchases overshadowed works of mercy that could at least sustain the poor: those who pay for indulgences yet pass by needy persons buy one thing and one thing only—the wrath of God.[17] In his fiftieth thesis the political and financial significance of the indulgence trade comes into sight. Albrecht, the archbishop of Magdeburg and member of the noble Hohenzollern family, wanted to be named archbishop of Mainz. Yet such a dual appointment was not appropriate: the church insisted on one bishop in one diocese, not one bishop with two dioceses. To help the Roman curia overlook this irregularity, Albrecht borrowed a considerable sum of money from the Fugger banking family in Augsburg, Germany. In turn he agreed to hand over half of the indulgence profits as payment on his loan; the other half would be sent to Rome for the rebuilding of St. Peter's.

Figure 2.4. Lucas Cranach, *The pope oversees indulgence sales,* 1521, from the "Passional Christi und Antichristi."

While Luther did not mention and perhaps did not know of the loan repayment plan, he was aware of the project to rebuild St. Peter's: "Christians are to be taught that if the pope knew the exactions of the indulgence preachers, he would rather that the basilica of St. Peter were burned to ashes than built up with the skin, flesh, and bones of his sheep."[18] Here we gain the impression that the pope was unaware of the manner in which indulgences were being sold in Germany. Yet toward the end of the theses, Luther asked, "Why doesn't the pope, whose wealth today is greater than the wealth of the richest [of ancient Romans], build this one basilica . . . with his own money rather than with the money of poor believers?"[19] Can one sense here a note of resistance to Roman Church taxes levied on the German people? Perhaps. After all Luther was both awestruck and revolted by the gaping disparity between the opulent magnificence of the papal court and the desperate misery of Rome's many impoverished citizens during his visit to the city in 1510.

Wandering the streets of Rome, Luther was an unknown monk from a section of Germany that was among the last to be christianized, a "troublesome" province in the eyes of the Roman papal court. One wonders, then, what was going through his mind on October 31, 1517, as he sent a copy of his theses to Albrecht, the new archbishop of Mainz and the man who had hired Johannes Tetzel to sell indulgences in the diocese bordering Wittenberg. Did he imagine that the archbishop and the indulgence preacher would come to the university for a sip of schnapps and a cordial debate with the faculty? It mattered not. By December of that year, Albrecht had forwarded the document to Pope Leo X. Within a few days, every member of the papal household knew the German monk's name and wanted him silenced.

Economic Implications of a Theological Critique

What Roman church officials could not have imagined was the degree to which Luther's critique of the commercialization of spiritual "treasures" would capture the imagination of the many who believed that far too many priests, bishops, monks, and friars had become "thieves and bandits" in the sheepfold of Christ (John 10:8). Indeed, one hears faintly yet persistently throughout the theses the sentiment already alive in much of Christian Europe: instead of protecting the most vulnerable members of the flock, the shepherds were actually devouring the sheep. "Mother Church was now perceived by many as 'smothering' Church. . . . The true poor were contrasted with the poverty of the monks, 'those idle, rich, fat beggars, who ride on great horses.' "[20] One quite popular cartoon from the period shows an obese monk revealed as a wolf eating the food and house of a widow and child who stand small and thin at his side, their hands open in supplication. It is no

Figure 2.5. *Widow and child beg before a gluttonous monk-wolf,* late 15th/ early 16th c., a German or Swiss cartoon mocking monastic wealth.

small thing that Luther the monk, raised in a peasant household, was conscious of those who were "perched precariously on the edge of poverty" and equally aware of the great disparity between wealthy church "shepherds" and the many "sheep" who held out their hands in search of mercy and in need of bread. Perhaps to an older Luther or to contemporary Lutheran and Protestant ears, the young monk who wrote the theses sounds a little too "medieval" when he sternly notes that those who ignore the needy and spend their coins on church parchment purchase nothing but the wrath of God or when he counsels every Christian to turn away from indulgences and participate in messy and often difficult corporal works of mercy: feeding the hungry, giving drink to the thirsty, clothing the naked, sheltering the homeless, visiting the sick, and ransoming the captives (Matt. 25:34-36). Oh my, all those good works!

There was more at work here, however, than the simple exhortation to prefer works of mercy to indulgences. Some would be quick to claim that the public criticism printed and circulated in the theses was simply a prelude to the subsequent and more "significant" debate over papal authority and the role of church councils in adjudicating ecclesial disputes or that Luther simply voiced a common complaint concerning religious practices already heard throughout much of Europe. Clearly there is some truth in those claims. Yet there may be another and complementary dimension of the criticism that merits attention.

Is it not possible that we hear in the denunciation of sales strategies applied to spiritual "treasures" an early "evangelical" criticism of the late medieval response to the urgent quest for salvation? Luther would write that "the true treasure of the church is the most holy gospel of the glory and grace of God."[21] Yet the assertion begs the question, what was meant by "gospel" or "grace"? Luther's predecessors, the medieval theologians, spoke of grace as a divinely given energizing force, mediated through the sacraments, a power that could transform humans so that they would love God and others.[22] Yet one gains the distinct impression that by the early sixteenth century, this notion of grace as a substantive, transforming power had become *quantified*: one could obtain more of it, one could receive, as it were, more "graces." Greater effort could produce greater measurable results. Perhaps this understanding of grace as spiritual quantity emerged through popular consciousness, a poorly trained clergy, a new trend in theology, or the influence of emerging capitalism. Regardless of its sources, in an environment that allowed the quantification of spiritual realities, it would not be difficult to imagine the sacraments or the many sacramentals of the church[23] as "things" that one could accumulate.

The scholastic theologians of the thirteenth century, who viewed grace as a sanctifying power in human life, did not intend their theology to be translated crassly into a "quantification" of salvation. Yet the language of late medieval Christianity, embedded in Luther's theses, expressed and sanctioned such a "commoditization" by drawing on economic metaphors: spiritual penalties could be paid (22), so much money clinking in a chest released so many souls from purgatory (27), one could buy privileges related to the sacraments (35), the pope could make a withdrawal on the reserve fund (i.e., treasury) of Christ's merits (56), and funeral or anniversary masses for the dead could be purchased (88). Roman Catholic Church historian Josef Lortz has pointed out that "by the sixteenth-century, the upper classes in many northern German cities were endowing altars and anniversary masses for the dead in such great quantity that *the priests were incapable of keeping up with the demand.*"[24] In this "spiritualized economy" the practice of accumulating spiritual "capital" would seem quite normal. In the late medieval search to "secure an insecure existence,"[25] wouldn't the securing of such capital or investments actually help one obtain an eternal retirement with all the redeemed? Now, wrote Luther, the church fishes for the wealth of men.[26]

Only three years after publishing the theses, Luther would suggest that "[they] have turned the holy sacrament [of the Mass] into mere merchandise, a market, and a profit-making business."[27] It would seem that the commercialization of spiritual realities could actually produce competition for such "goods and services" rather than a "communion," a free sharing of treasures or gifts.[28] Thus, we come to the difficulty, the terrible difficulty with such a spiritual economy: in the competition for "goods and services"—either spiritual or material—the privileged always benefit while the poor and the needy usually lose. In the pursuit of spiritual capital "it is certain that greed and avarice increase." By drawing attention to the poor (43); the needy person (45); the skin, flesh, and bones of Christ's sheep (50); those who are cajoled (51); poor believers (86); and the largely unlearned laity (90) within the context of an argument over theological practices, Luther raised into relief the spiritual-economic transactions of late medieval Christianity and diagnosed their deleterious effects. In that social world, where the ancient Roman patronage practice of *do ut des*—"I give so that you give to me in return"—still exerted enormous influence (consider Albrecht's "gift" to the curia), one could begin to see the dynamic of a spiritual system that mirrored an economic one. In that world those who worked hard would be rewarded, those who invested wisely would reap benefits, and those who competed aggressively would succeed, that is, of course, if they had the means to do so.

The problem, however, was this: in the effort to accumulate greater and greater amounts of spiritual capital, one's attention was drawn to this world only to the degree that work "here" would benefit one "there," in the world to come. What, then, of the poor, the needy person, the unlearned, and the easily cajoled? Here is the tragic irony: in a spiritual-economic system that actually rewarded personal charity, the poor were *absolutely necessary* to the dispenser of charity. The burgher, the prince, and the businessperson relied upon and *needed* the widow, the orphan, and the beggar in order to act charitably and gain spiritual assets. "If giving alms helped to wash away sin, then helping the poor was a way for the wealthy to gain salvation."[29] Little thought was given to changing the conditions in which the poor lived or the assumptions that sanctioned a permanent class of hungry people. Their purpose was to afford *others* the opportunity to be charitable.[30]

From the perspective of the poor, however, from the "underside" of history, how could the widow, the orphan, or the hungry poor participate in the market economy of late medieval Christianity? What use was the money chest filled with indulgences if one had no coin? And if, for instance, a poor widow possessed only one coin, would she spend it on a piece of paper that she was told would contribute to her eternal destiny or on the piece of bread her hungry child desperately needed?

One might say that Luther pressed his hand to the rapid pulse of late medieval Christianity and diagnosed a pervasive anxiety concerning human destiny. Perhaps the rapidity of the pulse symbolized a series of questions about one's eternal destiny that may be difficult for modern ears, at least modern Protestant ears, to hear: Will I have participated sufficiently with the grace of Christ to ensure a merciful judgment on that great and dreaded day? Will I suffer the torment of eternal estrangement from my loved ones and my Creator? What more might I do? But what if I, disabled soldier, impoverished peasant, or widow with children, can do nothing more? What if I cannot find the pfennig to invest in the paper that might—just might—promise union with God and my children? At the same time Luther the monk witnessed the manner in which some monks—charged with charitable work among the homeless and the hungry—actually gobbled up what little material solace was at hand for the poor. In a culture focused on the life of the world to come, one might have hoped that the shepherds of the earthly flock would have taken to heart the words of the psalm chanted every year in every monastery, convent, and papal chapel throughout the Christian West: "Father of orphans and protector of widows is God in his holy habitation" (Ps. 68:5). But, then, in a spiritual economy that needed the poor as objects of charity but could not imagine them seated next to a plump burgher and his wife, maybe the market and its quantifiable logic simply overwhelmed the disruptive power of ancient words waiting to be heard anew.

3
BUYING SPIRITUAL GOODS AND SERVICES

The Social Implications of Justification by Grace

Whether Martin Luther posted a series of theses on the door of a Wittenberg church on October 31, 1517, remains an open question. It is clear, however, that he sent a copy of the document to Albrecht, the archbishop of Mainz, and that his religious superiors in the Augustinian Order of Hermits were well aware of the document's content. Some estimates suggest that more than twenty thousand copies of the theses, quickly translated into German, were printed and distributed throughout much of the region in November and December of 1517. Within a short period of time, the unknown biblical scholar from a small-town university had become a household name.

Yet with fame came controversy. Many welcomed the theses and soon began calling Luther *die Wittenbergisch Nachtigall*, the Wittenberg nightingale, singing loudly to the approach of sunrise from the midst of night's darkness.[1] Others viewed him as a loose cannon, a precocious upstart who should have kept his "academic" debate within the university's stone walls. Under a cloud of conflict, the superiors of the German Augustinians asked him to lead a discussion of the theses at Heidelberg during the general chapter of the order. On Monday, April 26, 1518, Luther presented a set of forty theological and philosophical theses at the chapter meeting. Following the theses Luther added twenty-eight comments. The "proofs," as they were called, set forth his emerging theology. Here one can discern his skepticism of human works contributing to salvation (e.g., indulgences) and his suspicion of the medieval use of philosophy in the construction of Christian

theology (e.g., Aristo-
tle). Luther's inter-
pretation of the New
Testament letters of
Paul, "the chosen ves-
sel and instrument of
Christ,"[2] inspired him
to promote a series of
theological claims that
called into question
the achievement of
medieval theology. In
particular he took issue
with the medieval argu-
ment that one could
come to the knowledge
of God through the
observation of God's
"handiwork," the natu-
ral world. On the con-
trary, argued Luther,

Figure 3.1. 1. Hans Sachs, *The Wittenberg Nightingale*, 1523, the title page of Sachs' poem in praise of Luther.

one could come to the knowledge of God only through Jesus Christ, his humanity, and his humiliating suffering on the cross. The pre-eminent Christian revelation, Luther argued, was to be found neither in the order of creation, as good and beautiful as that might be, nor in philosophy even when that wisdom was brought to the service of Christian theology. All too easily, Luther claimed, trust in human phi-losophy would eclipse or distort the central proclamation of Christi-anity. The primary revelation, he argued, is God's open embrace of human suffering as recognized in the humbled and suffering Christ. "Because [humans] misused the knowledge of God through works, God wished again to be recognized in suffering, and to condemn wis-dom concerning invisible things by means of wisdom concerning vis-ible things, so that those who did not honor God as manifested in his works [e.g., creation] should honor him as he is hidden in his suffering."[3]

Next to the potent medieval images of God as the transcendent ruler of the universe or the just judge of the living and the dead, Luther placed the image of a vulnerable and abandoned human being left to die outside the city gates, at considerable distance from the centers of economic and political power—the market and the court—as well as the center of religious power where conventional wisdom expected the Messiah to return: the steps of the temple in Jerusalem. "Now it is not sufficient for anyone, and it does him no good to recognize God in his glory and majesty, unless he recognizes him in the humility and shame of the cross. Thus God destroys the wisdom of the wise. As Isaiah [45:15] says, 'Truly, you are a God who hides himself.' "[4]

Between the words one can hear Luther's own anguished participation in the late medieval quest for salvation, his fear of standing before a righteous judge who, he believed, would readily condemn him to an eternity of dark isolation and torment. Within the words, however, one can recognize the christocentric, Christ-focused, nature of his budding theological project. Of course, Luther was not the first Western theologian to focus on the suffering Christ as a protest against the jurid-

Figure 3.2. 2. H. Schaeufelein, *Crucifixion with open tomb*, 1519, from an early sermon by Luther on the holy suffering of Christ.

ical image of Christ as the judge of the living and the dead, the sword of justice and the lily of mercy issuing forth from his mouth, an image painted and inscribed throughout much of medieval Europe. In the thirteenth century it was Francis of Assisi who claimed that the crucified Christ spoke to him and invited him to identify with the poor and hungry. During the middle of the fourteenth century, as Europe reeled from the ever-mounting death toll of the Black Plague, Christians turned to the image of the suffering Christ with whom they could identify as they suffered from a plague that struck down poor and wealthy, the innocent and the wicked alike. Indeed, it was Luther's mentor, the Augustinian Johann von Staupitz, who encouraged the young monk, obsessed with God's justice and wrath, to attach himself to Christ and Christ's wounds, for there he would find mercy. For Staupitz and Luther, however, attachment to the suffering Christ was not one more thing one could do to please an angry father figure. Rather, the suffering Christ was the tangible embodiment of mercy and, consequently, God's grace.

Mindful of the late medieval search for salvation, Luther began the process of critiquing the very notion of *quest*, as if salvation were primarily a human responsibility aided by the sacraments, sacramentals, and charitable works promoted by the church. In the presence of the "self-giving" of God, revealed and offered to humanity in the life and suffering of Christ, moral achievement meant nothing. "He who has not been brought low, reduced to nothing through the cross and suffering, takes credit for works and wisdom and does not give credit to God. He thus misuses and defiles the gifts of God."[5] In the spiritual-economic milieu of late medieval Christian culture, a system that promoted religious patronage and charity, Luther argued that such works would actually lead the Christian to expect, if not demand, something from God: "I have given to you, now you give to me." In his eyes, this was sheer blasphemy. How could any creature make such a demand upon the Creator?

In contrast to this way of thinking, Luther marshaled a formidable array of quotations from the letters of Paul centered on the powerful word *justification*, on being made right with God by God:

> For the righteousness of God is not acquired by means of acts frequently repeated, as Aristotle taught, but it is imparted by faith, for "He who through faith is righteous shall live" (Rom. 1[:17]). . . . Therefore I wish to have the words "without work" understood in the following manner: Not that the righteous person does nothing, but that his works do not make him righteous, rather that his righteousness creates works. For *grace and faith are infused without our works. After they have been imparted the works follow.* . . . "For we

hold that man is justified by faith apart from works of law" (Rom. 3[:28]). In other words, works contribute nothing to justification. . . . Justification by faith in Christ is sufficient. . . . Christ is his wisdom, righteousness, etc., as I Cor. 1[:30] has it, that he himself may be Christ's action and instrument.[6]

With the image of the self-giving God who actively embraces human suffering—recognized in the crucified Christ—Luther countered the late medieval notion that one could move *toward God* by holding a correct belief, by meritorious actions or charitable works, by offering one's suffering to God, or by having faith understood as a humanly created disposition toward God. None of these things were of any value insofar as they made one pleasing to God. Instead, Luther insisted that any and all salvific movement originated in God and advanced *toward human beings*, a movement revealed preeminently in the birth, life, death, and resurrection of Christ.

Rather than seeking its own good, the love of God flows forth and bestows good. Therefore sinners are attractive because they are loved; they are not loved because they are attractive. . . . Thus Christ says: "For I came not to call the righteous, but sinners" [Matt. 9:13]. This is the love of the cross, born of the cross, which turns in the direction where it does not find good which it may enjoy, but where it may confer good upon the bad and needy person.[7]

Figure 3.3. *Mary Magdalene before the Holy Trinity,* 1518, from the title page of a tract on the love of God, written by Luther's mentor, Johann von Staupitz.

The medieval teaching that humans could cooperate with the grace of Christ and perform meritorious works that would contribute to their salvation was rejected. At the same time such a rejection was a de facto repudiation of the entire spiritual-economic system that had emerged so strongly in the late medieval period.

Christ Coming to the Christian

One year later, on Palm Sunday, Luther preached on the second (epistle) reading appointed in the medieval lectionary for the liturgy that commemorates the entrance of Jesus into Jerusalem. The text was Philippians 2:5-11, the early liturgical hymn quoted by Paul in his letter to the Christian community at Philippi:

> Let the same mind be in you that was in Christ Jesus,
>> who, though he was in the form of God,
>>> did not regard equality with God
>>> as something to be exploited,
>> but emptied himself,
>>> taking the form of a slave,
>>> being born in human likeness.
>> And being found in human form,
>>> he humbled himself
>>> and became obedient to the point of death—
>>> even death on a cross.
>
>> Therefore God also highly exalted him
>>> and gave him the name
>>> that is above every name,
>> so that at the name of Jesus
>>> every knee should bend,
>>> in heaven and on earth and under the earth,
>> and every tongue should confess
>>> that Jesus Christ is Lord,
>>> to the glory of God the Father.

In his reflection upon this hymn, a text to which Luther would return time and again throughout his career as if the hymn were the keystone of his Christology, he set forth his understanding of "justification by grace," that teaching in which, he insisted, there was to be no compromise. At the outset of his sermon, Luther made a distinction between two kinds of "righteousness," a powerful symbol that signified a "right" relationship between God and humanity. The first he called an "alien righteousness," alien in the sense that it comes from another and is given to a person; "alien" because one cannot claim this righteousness as one's own creation. It is not "natural" to humanity but rather is freely given by another. "This is the righteousness of Christ by which he justifies through faith."[8] This first and alien righteousness—this being made right with God—"is given to [people] in baptism and whenever [they] are truly repentant."[9] We are reminded of the claim Luther made at the Heidelberg chapter meeting: "Grace and faith are infused without our works." Thus, Luther and his reforming colleagues would not stray from the medieval practice of baptizing newborn infants because the vulnerability and utter dependence of an infant on his or her parents correlated with Luther's Christian anthropology, his understanding of the human person as utterly dependent on the mercy of God as someone who could bring no bargaining chips to the table and therefore make no demands upon the Creator based on personal achievements.

Luther's anthropology, however, did not focus solely on human dependence. Luther's emphasis on humanity as vulnerable and in need of God's mercy arose out of what he considered a prior condition into which every human being was born, the condition of sin. Having mentioned the term, let us pause for a moment and be mindful that a variety of Christian anthropologies[10] were already present and newly emerging in the sixteenth century. Luther's understanding of the "sinful condition" departed from the popular notion of sin as the willful breaking of God's commandments or the laws of the church; that is, sin as disobedience to law. While he recognized that humans *do* break laws, such disobedience was a symptom of something deeper. He also broke with the medieval scholastic notion of sin as a lack of grace in creatures seriously wounded by the Fall—that is, sin as deprivation with dire consequences. For Luther humanity was marked by an exclusive focus on the self to the exclusion of God and of others, what he called *incurvatus in se*, turned inward on the self. "It is easy, if we use any diligence at all . . . to understand how . . . we seek our fulfillment and love ourselves, how we are turned in upon ourselves and become ingrown at least in our heart, even when we cannot sense it in our actions."[11] Indeed, at times he spoke of this being "ingrown" as a form of oppression, of being in bondage to evil forces.[12] Yet Luther was not content to view the human condition as one marked by mere selfishness. "Our nature has been so deeply curved in upon itself because of the viciousness of original sin that it not only turns the finest gifts of God in upon itself and enjoys them . . . it even uses God to achieve these aims, but it also seems to be ignorant of this very fact, that in acting so iniquitously . . . it is even seeking God for its own sake."[13]

As if this inward curvature were a centripetal force, Luther argued that it would pull everything, consciously and unconsciously, into the orbit of the self, using others, the gifts of God, and even God to support the self as the one true "subject" in a universe of its own making. In such a state, God and others become objectified, deprived of their own unique character as other "subjects." From this perspective no wonder the poor and the hungry could be perceived as necessary "objects" who served the charitable and self-centered interests of the almsgivers. The value of the recipient of charitable assistance, Luther seemed to argue, was utilitarian: the poor were useful to the goals of the charitable donor. The hungry poor were simply there *to assist the donor* in his or her charitable giving, a work that would be counted in the donor's favor. Oh, yes, the hungry poor were valuable, remarkably valuable, in a spiritual system that awarded donors spiritual points for their generosity. Yet was the hungry person, the widow, or the orphan viewed as a vital subject in the world, as something other than the living "container" in which charitable persons could make a deposit that would reap rewards elsewhere?

Luther claimed that in contrast to the powerful centrifugal force in human life, the reception of "alien righteousness" effectively broke the stranglehold of sin as *incurvatus in se* and began the process of turning the inward-focused person outward toward God and others, in particular, the neighbor in need.

> This alien righteousness, instilled in us without our works by grace alone—while the Father, to be sure, inwardly draws us to Christ—is set opposite original sin, likewise alien, which we acquire without our

works by birth alone. Christ daily drives out the old Adam more and more in accordance with the extent to which faith and knowledge of Christ grow. For alien righteousness is not instilled all at once, but it begins, makes progress, and is finally perfected at the end through death.[14]

For Luther this turning outward in faith to God and in love to one's neighbor was effected by union with Christ: "Everything which Christ has is ours, graciously bestowed on us unworthy [people] out of God's sheer mercy."[15] Here Luther invoked the image of a marriage in which the spouses "have all things in common because they are one." In this relationship there is a mutual sharing between Christ and the newly baptized Christian; Christ withholds none of his gifts: "Christ's righteousness and all that he has becomes ours; rather, he himself becomes ours."[16]

That modest nuance—"he himself becomes ours"—is significant. Here Luther underscored what has been overlooked or dismissed by his commentators: as the Word of God did not scorn humanity but emptied itself into human form, so that same Word of God, the life-giving Spirit who is Christ, effects union and dwells within the baptized and justified Christian.[17] "God justifies by *imputing* righteousness from outside us. Justification by faith is a relation, not a substantial amalgamation."[18] In his critique of the quantification of grace (or any spiritual reality, for that matter), Luther suggested that "jus-

Figure 3.4. *Christ surrounded by angels writes on justification before St. Paul who is composing the letter to the Galatians,* 1695, from the title page of a 17th c. edition of the Bible.

tification by grace" could hold not only a legal or existential meaning (i.e., forgiveness of the sinner) but also a relational meaning marked by an intimate, spousal sharing (i.e., union with Christ).

The intent of the teaching on justification by grace was to exclude—to "drown," "kill," and "condemn"—any notion that one could do or believe anything that would make one pleasing to God and thus merit God's grace. It was intended to reverse the commonly held notion that one's life on this earth was to be spent in active preparation for the last judgment, the life of the world to come. In a moral world marked by rewards and punishments, Luther suggested that being a good, hard-working person would not help one in terms of salvation. By situating the act of justification at baptism, no less at the baptism of a passive infant, Luther in effect placed the promise of salvation, rather than the search for salvation, at *the beginning* of a Christian's life rather than at its end. Even before a child could pray, receive the sacraments, feed the hungry, buy an indulgence, purchase a mass, or endow a church, that is, before he or she could cooperate with the grace of Christ, "righteousness [was] given in baptism." But while the initial intent of the central teaching on justification was, on the one hand, to thwart the human drive to move toward God and, on the other, to highlight the movement of God toward humanity, a movement marked by the bestowal of God's mercy and unconditional grace upon humanity—that is, while its intention was to touch and calm the anxious nerve of late medieval Christians, to speak to them theologically and existentially—the teaching also held another implication: there could be no condition or status in life that merited greater spiritual favor than any other. If the housewife, the pope, the burgher, the peasant, the soldier, and the orphan were all captured from the moment of birth by the inward turn on the self, then neither gender nor race, neither socioeconomic status nor religious profession could help one escape that condition. Neither status nor socioeconomic class could serve as the grounds for any "entitlement" to any spiritual privilege. As would become clear in his critique of the two estates that divided medieval society into a "religious" class (monks, priests, nuns) and a "secular" class (princes, farmers, artisans), [19] the former could make no claim to greater holiness than the latter. While the spiritual-economic system of late medieval Christianity encouraged the bishop or the prince to act charitably toward the hungry widow, such charity, argued Luther, meant nothing and accrued nothing in terms of one's justification by God. In a community of spiritual equals, there was to be only this: mutual concern and service.

The Christian Turning to the Neighbor

If one were freed from spending one's life in preparation for the life of the world to come, if one no longer had to look "heavenward," if one no longer had to be anxious over the degree to which one had cooperated with the grace of Christ, the Christian was then free to attend to life in *this world.* Without diminishing or ignoring the transcendent nature of God or the divinity of Christ, Luther's understanding of justification and its deeply christological center inspired him to embrace the humanity of Jesus. In the suffering of the psalmist, voiced by Jesus of Nazareth in his humiliating crucifixion, Luther found existential identification. In his own terrifying anxiety and sense of abandonment, he came to realize that he was neither alone nor left to what he experienced as the anger of God at sinners. This point of identification was not made with the unseen and overwhelming power of divinity, but rather with the one who emerged from the pages of the New Testament, the one, according to the early Christian hymn, who "did not regard equality with God as something to be exploited, but emptied himself, taking the form of a slave, being born in human likeness" (Phil. 2:6-7). "Whatever [Christ] did," Luther said in his Palm Sunday sermon, "he did it for us and desired to be ours, saying, 'I am among you as one who serves' [Luke 22:27]."[20]

If the movement toward God and the anxious gaze heavenward were reversed by the continuing advance of a merciful God who would justify a vulnerable infant, that movement continued in and through the baptized who were free to live in this world as the "sacrament" of the living Christ, to engage this world as Christ had engaged his own world. As Lindberg notes, "Because salvation [was] now perceived as the foundation of life rather than the goal and achievement of life, the energy and resources poured into acquiring other-worldly capital [could] now be redirected to this-worldly activities."[21] The movement into the world was effected, Luther claimed, by another righteousness distinguished but not separated from the first and "alien" righteous-ness. "The second kind of righteousness is our proper righteousness, not because we alone work it, but because we work with that first and alien righteousness. This is that manner of life spent profitably in good works. . . . This righteousness consists in love to one's neighbor."[22] Luther had already argued that the baptized and justified Christian was made one with the living Christ: "[The one] who trusts in Christ exists in Christ . . . is one with Christ, having the same righteousness."[23] Yet the image of Christ that sparked his imagination was the one set forth in the early Christian hymn, the one who emptied himself into human-ity and took the form of a servant.

This was a remarkable claim to make in the first and sixteenth cen-

Figure 3.5. Lucas Cranach, *Christ heals a poor man while the pope is entertained by jousters,* 1521, from the "Passional Christi und Antichristi."

turies. In his sociological study of the rise of Christianity in the ancient Mediterranean, Rodney Stark notes:

> To anyone raised in a Judeo-Christian or Islamic culture, the pagan gods seem almost trivial. Each is but one of a host of gods and godlings of very limited scope, power, and concern. Moreover, they

seem quite morally deficient. They do terrible things to one another, and sometimes they play ugly pranks on humans. But, for the most part, they appear to pay little attention to things "down below." The simple phrase "For God so loved the world . . ." would have puzzled an educated pagan. And the notion that the gods care how we treat one another would have been dismissed as patently absurd.[24]

The claim that a powerful deity actually demonstrates care for humanity would have jeopardized the very "power" of a deity. That the gods make demands upon or expect sacrifices from humans was well known, but "care" for humanity? In the ancient world women and slave nurses, both considered inferior to "powerful" and public males, were expected to demonstrate affection for their offspring, something welcomed, perhaps, yet a sign of their inherent "weakness." To suggest that one was "in the form of God" but emptied himself, "taking the form of a slave" —that divine power would appear to humans in the form of a slave or servant—would have seemed utterly ludicrous.[25] That this god and this god's "offspring" or "son" were marked by mercy for humanity, especially the most vulnerable of human beings, only would have underscored the novelty and seemingly inherent weakness of this movement named after an executed criminal. "Classical philosophers," continues Stark, "regarded mercy and pity as pathological emotions—defects of character to be avoided by all rational [people] . . . [a] defect of character unworthy of the wise. . . . [Indeed] Plato had removed the problem of beggars from his ideal state by dumping them over its borders."[26]

Here is the irony that Luther and many others discerned in the sixteenth century: at the heart of church leadership was enshrined the image of the servant. In fact, the bishop of Rome referred to himself as the *Servus Servorum Dei*—"the servant of the servants of God." Yet this "servant" spoke, acted, dressed, and exercised his considerable authority in a manner that had more in common with a powerful and wealthy secular monarch than the poor, wandering, and property-less Christ whose vicar he claimed to be.[27] In this religious and political context, Luther's focus on Christ the servant was a recovery of the paradoxical force of the gospel parables and Pauline insight, a recovery that set forth the manner in which personal or communal power was

to be exercised in light of the gospel. The promotion of the image
of the servant was a protest against religious leadership exercised in a
manner that had little in common with image of the earthly Christ.
Christian leaders appeared to have more in common with monarchs
and wealthy businesspersons than with the Christ who was at home
among the hungry, the poor, and the sick. That word *servant*, so powerful a symbol in Luther's imagination, correlated with his insistence,
expressed during the Heidelberg Disputation, that the invisible God
reveals God's self and God's power to humanity in weakness, in suffering, in those experiences where conventional wisdom would least
expect a powerful deity to be present. This is to say that divine power
was broken, not only in the humiliation of an ignominious death,[28]
but also in the manner in which that power was exercised socially:
"[Christ] was pre-eminent in such attributes as are particularly proper
to the form of God. Yet he was not haughty in that form; he did not
please himself (Rom. 15:3); nor did he disdain and despise those who
were enslaved and subjected to various evils . . . although he was free,
he made himself servant of all."[29]

From this perspective power does not "trickle down" as it would
in a hierarchical structure, becoming less frequent and consequently
less effective as it comes close to the base. Rather, power is exercised
or shared at the lowest level among those who are most in need.
"Through the figure of the members of the body, Paul teaches in
Romans 12[:4-5] and 1 Corinthians 12[:12-27] how the strong, honorable, healthy members do not glory over those that are weak, less
honorable, and sick as if they were their masters and gods; but on
the contrary they serve them the more, forgetting their own honor,
health, and power."[30]

The "alien righteousness" received by the baptized and justified
Christian possesses a social form, what Luther called "proper righteousness." "This righteousness follows the example of Christ [the ser-
vant] in this respect [1 Peter 2:21] and is transformed into his likeness
(2 Cor. 3:18). *It is precisely this that Christ requires.* Just as he himself
did all things for us . . . so he desires that we also should set the same
example for our neighbors."[31] As Luther has made clear, this second
righteousness is not something that springs naturally or inherently
from even the justified person but, rather, is the consequence of the

first righteousness; one yields to the other, animates the other, the two never being confused.

The order of sequence and distinction between the two would be repeated three years later, in 1522, when Luther wrote an introduction to a series of model sermons for the church year. In his "Brief Instruction on What to Look for and Expect in the Gospels," he counseled the reader first to recognize Christ as a gift, "as a present that God has given you and that is your own. This means that when you see or hear of Christ doing or suffering something [in the Gospels], you do not doubt that Christ himself, with his deeds and suffering, belongs to you. . . . This is what it means to have a proper grasp of the gospel."[32] Here Luther asserted the teaching on justification, the gracious movement of God toward humanity. Yet there is a second way of reading and understanding Scripture that flows from the first one and should never precede it: "Now when you have Christ as the foundation . . . of your salvation, then the other

Figure 3.6. *Luther preaching the gospel with crucifix and Bible*, 1522, from a work on the piety of Christ by the reformer Johann Eberlin von Guenzburg.

part follows: that you take him as your example, giving yourself in service to your neighbor just as you see that Christ has given himself for you."[33] In contrast to late medieval spiritual directors who imagined the Christian life primarily as an *imitatio Christi* "that would make one pleasing to God,"[34] Luther reversed the order: the *donum Christi* gives birth to the *imitatio Christi*, the imitation flows from but does not produce the gift.

Because of the union between the living Christ and the Christian, effected through baptism and nourished in the Eucharist, the source of service, of good works, becomes the indwelling Christ who acts through the believer. This means at least two things. First, the Christian is not an automaton, a puppet controlled inwardly and even against his or her will by the living Christ. There is freedom in the exercise of service. Indeed, the inward pull toward the self and the self alone will be ever present: Christians will consistently fail in their care of the neighbor and the world. There should be little surprise in this claim, because the Christian, the creature, is not God.

In protest against a seemingly unfettered exaltation of human reason, a temptation he sensed in the lively humanism of his time, Luther asserted both the serious limits of reason and its God-given nature. With all other people Christians are marked by limited knowledge; they do not possess the mind of God. Consequently, their engagement in the world, while absolutely necessary and marked by real, tangible effects, will always be limited and provisional.[35] Yet the presence of grace and its centrifugal power moving outward to the neighbor and the world is ever present as well, nourished by the word of God, the sacraments of grace, and the baptized community through its mutual consolation and conversation. While the teaching on justification was intended to highlight first the movement of God toward humanity, the priority of "alien righteousness" in the lives of Christians, and the recognition of Christ as gift freely given, Luther's distinction between two forms of righteousness also brought into relief the necessary movement of Christians into the world, the exercise of "proper" or "social righteousness" in the service of the neighbor, and the call to imitate Christ the servant in daily life.

The Social Implications of the Teaching on Justification

Luther and his reforming colleagues at the University of Wittenberg would never depart from the primacy of the teaching on justification by grace. They considered it the "article of faith" on which everything stood firm or collapsed; there could be no vital and faithful Christianity without this biblical and theological principle as its foundation.[36] It should come as no surprise that Luther's focus on the metaphor of justification responded to his own spiritual anxiety.[37] The discovery of the meaning of the "righteousness of God" as it related to the "justification of the sinner by grace alone" spoke to him existentially, to the depths of his anxiety: "I felt that I was altogether born again and had entered paradise itself through open gates."[38]

We should note the manner in which Luther arrived at this primary insight. First, he was influenced by his own upbringing in a home where his father, Hans Luther, had worked diligently to move his family upward from their peasant origins to the enviable status of mine owners. Luther's father expected his son to become a lawyer, an achievement that would place him among the wealthy who could afford legal counsel. Luther was raised in an emerging economic system that made it possible for people without land or noble lineage to prosper financially through sheer labor and smart business practices. It was evident from the life of his father that hard work yielded results and rewards. Second, having ended his progress toward a legal profession, Luther entered one of the most rigorous of religious communities where strenuous ascetic discipline demonstrated one's love of God and growth in holiness.[39] In this regard the young Luther was influenced by the spiritual-economic world of late medieval Christianity, a world that offered a plethora of means for earnest Christians who sought to secure their salvation. Third, Luther was a student and a biblical scholar, a professor of theology. It was through his meticulous study of the Bible in preparation for his lectures, in particular his sometimes tortured examination of Paul's letters, that his personal anxiety was dispelled and he felt himself to be "born again," released from his anxious quest.

From his gradual recognition of the implications of the powerful symbol of "justification by grace," he began to question the foundations of the theological world he had inherited and inhabited. For Luther and the university colleagues who gravitated to his emerging theology, the Pauline metaphor of justification was not only the key to rethinking the existential, hermeneutical, theological, soteriological, sacramental, and ecclesial dimensions of Christianity,[40] it also became the key through which they responded to the communities and individuals who, having accepted Luther's teachings, were engaged in the pressing economic, political, and social issues of their time. If "justification by grace" was the key, the foundation, the center of the reform project, then *it was the key to everything*, not only God's relationship with humanity but also one's relationship with others in the world. And since life in this world is lived within the economic, political, and social fabrics of a particular culture, the "article" upon which everything stood or collapsed would possess economic, political, and social implications, or it would prove utterly irrelevant and, thus, useless.

Luther rejected the late medieval search for salvation and the spiritual-economic system that was intended to support Christians in that search. No work, no behavior, no purchase, no claim to spiritual privilege based on gender, class, education, or religious standing could secure one's eternal destiny. While the teaching on justification set forth the assertion that God justifies humanity apart from any and every kind of work, it also encoded a radical egalitarianism: all were caught in the centripetal field of sin and all could be liberated from that field by the word and action of Another. Perhaps it was release from the anxiety that attended such a quest and its inherent competitiveness that elicited criticism from those who supervised and benefited from the sale of spiritual "goods" and approval from those who accepted the notion that the accumulation of capital no longer mattered.

At the same time Luther's theology of grace as God's unmerited regard for humanity effectively criticized the notion that some persons—the hungry poor and the destitute—could be "used," even "charitably," for those who sought to advance their spiritual if not social standing with donations. Luther's sharp criticism of Christians who act as "masters and gods" in their treatment of the weak underscored a relational dynamic alive in German urban centers but also expressed the social utility of the teaching on justification, one that could subvert the tendency to value persons of another socioeconomic class only to the degree that they "received" goods (the hungry poor) or "offered" goods (the wealthy). If the needy were not to be used for spiritual gain, they were to be encountered as real persons with real needs.

4

A Peasant Becomes a Priest

On November 7, 1519, Martin Luther's writings were condemned in solemn assembly by the Faculty of Theology at the University of Louvain. Five months later, in March 1520, Luther received word that the University of Cologne had also condemned his writings. Shortly thereafter, the papal letter threatening Luther's excommunication was signed by Leo X and published in Rome on June 23. Johannes Eck, theologian at the University of Ingolstadt and zealous critic of Luther, was charged with disseminating the papal bull throughout Germany. Arriving as the bearer of threatening news and already disliked by many German humanists, Eck was met with protests, personal threats, and the destruction of the document. On December 10 the university students at Wittenberg sang the *Te Deum Laudamus* as Luther himself consigned the bull to the flames. Four weeks later he was excommunicated and declared a criminal in the Holy Roman Empire.

His expulsion from the church occurred only three years and a few months after the publication of his Ninety-five Theses. In that short period of time, the unknown university professor from a small German town had been transformed into a polarizing figure, one who attracted both adulation and acrimony throughout all of Europe. Little wonder: Luther was no diplomat. In June 1520 he wrote: "Farewell, unhappy, hopeless, blasphemous Rome! The wrath of God has come upon you in the end. . . . We have cared for Babylon and she is not healed. Let us then leave her that she may be the habitation of dragons, specters, ghosts, and witches . . . an idol of avarice, perfidy, apostasy, of cynics,

43

lechers, robbers, sorcerers, and endless other impudent monsters, a new pantheon of wickedness."[1]

Such sentiments would not go far in promoting fruitful dialogue and greater understanding of the call to reform heard throughout all of Western Christianity. On the other hand, the papal bull condemning Luther's writings and demanding his renunciation was no exercise in reconciliation.

> Arise, O Lord, and judge your own cause. Remember your reproaches to those who are filled with foolishness all through the day. Listen to our prayers, for foxes have

Figure 4.1. Lucas Cranach, *The pope as the whore of Babylon,* 1522, from Luther's German translation of the New Testament.

> arisen seeking to destroy the vineyard whose winepress you alone have trod. When you were about to ascend to your Father, you committed the care, rule, and administration of the vineyard, an image of the triumphant church, to Peter, as the head and your vicar and his successors. The wild boar from the forest seeks to destroy it and every wild beast feeds upon it.[2]

The "wild boar" from the dark Thuringian forests only grew in his animosity toward the Roman curia and its representatives in Germany. In Luther's mind they were incapable of reforming the church in light of the teaching on justification by grace. The German nation itself, said the threatening reprimand, was both a "frivolous" and "illustrious" country where this "plague and cancerous disease" had sprung to life. Yet Luther would soon be hailed in his native land as the ancient prophet Elias sprung to life and the *Hercules Germanicus* bashing Aristotle, Thomas

Aquinas, and Peter Lombard with a saw-toothed club, both a biblical prophet and a German hero.[3]

By May 1520 Luther's exasperation with Rome compelled him to turn toward the leaders of his "illustrious" nation: "I should be truly glad if kings, princes, and all nobles would take hold, and turn the knaves from Rome out of the country. . . . Out of our poverty we must enrich the ass-drivers and stable boys, nay, the harlots and knaves at Rome who look upon us as fools."[4] Encouraged by his university colleagues and members of the Saxon court, he completed a small booklet by mid-June, addressed to the emperor and the German nobility, asking them to begin the reform of the church.[5] That the German people claimed grievances, *gravamina*, concerning church abuses, was nothing new; lists of needed church reforms had been compiled for more than a hundred years and presented at imperial diets. Luther, however, prefaced his list of twenty-seven reform initiatives with a theological critique of three Roman claims that blocked reform: the division of the church into two orders, one holding rights over the other; the interpretation of Scripture as a papal or magisterial prerogative; and the curial claim that no one other than the pope could call a general council. The first printing numbered four thousand copies. A second run was quickly prepared once the first had been exhausted. It would prove to be a work with far-reaching consequences in the West, a work, nonetheless, that expressed a remarkable irony: the Augustinian monk who left "the world" for the hidden life of the cloister was urging "worldly" rulers to reform, to turn on its head, the very institution that had sanctioned his monastic calling.

Baptism Consecrates a Peasant as a Priest

Luther's first critique, an implication of his teaching on justification by grace, called into question the medieval division of Christianity into two "estates," a class made up of religious "professionals" (priests, bishops, monks, friars, and nuns) and another class filled with the laity (peasants, farmers, artisans, rulers, soldiers). In the stratified construction of sanctity in the late medieval world, to enter the former was to participate in a holy if not holier life, one at least popularly perceived as being closer to God. If the teaching on justification implied equality between all persons caught in sin and freed by grace, the distinction of the two "estates" was illusory. "All Christians are truly of the spiritual estate," wrote Luther, "and there is no difference among them except that of office."[6]

In effect Luther was promoting an early criticism of a hierarchically structured church that claimed to be the visible manifestation of Christ's body in the world. In the address Luther once again drew upon the New Testament to argue his case: the sacrament of baptism initiates a person into the one "spiritual estate" in which there exists a fundamental unity and equality between all the baptized members: "We are all consecrated priests through baptism, as St. Peter says in I Peter 2[:19], 'You are a royal priesthood and priestly realm.' The Apocalypse says, '[You have] made us to be priests and kings by [your] blood' [Rev. 5:9-10]."[7] Three realities make and unite all Christians in the one estate: "We have one baptism, one gospel, one faith, and are all equally Christians; for baptism, gospel, and faith alone make us spiritual and a Christian people."[8]

Figure 4.2. Workshop of Lucas Cranach, *Baptism,* 1545, from the title page of the section on baptism in Luther's "Small Catechism."

The corollary to Luther's earlier criticism of a stratified spiritual-economic "system" was this attack on a divided ("two estates") and stratified (hierarchically ordered) construction of the Christian community. Here we find the genesis of Luther's teaching on the universal priesthood of all the baptized. The "pyramid" of a stratified community was effectively flattened into a "circle" of the baptized in which there was no greater or lesser consecration than baptism, a sacramental consecration that effected union with Christ and the Christian community: "Christ does not have two different bodies, one temporal, the other spiritual.

There is but one Head [Christ] and one body [the church]."[9] The rituals of priestly ordination, monastic consecration, and papal investiture added nothing to one's spiritual status in this community.[10] His use of the New Testament image of a "priestly people" consecrated in baptism—a paradoxical and metaphorical image ("How can a peasant be a 'priest' and yet remain a peasant?")—allowed Luther to promote what he considered a critical biblical understanding of the church and launch an appeal to the largely baptized population of Germany. Thus, Luther asserted that "whoever comes out of the water of baptism can boast that he is already consecrated priest, bishop, and pope."[11] Would not the paradox—"an infant a bishop"—sound utterly ludicrous in the ears of Albrecht, the archbishop of Mainz?

Luther's insistence that the church is a "priestly" assembly (*Gemeinde*) consecrated through the baptismal ritual led him to claim that authority to select leaders for the community rests with the members of the community, not a group of leaders (e.g., the hierarchy) set over and above the Christian assembly: "Because we are all priests of equal standing, no one must push himself forward and take it upon himself, without our consent and election, to do that for which we all have equal authority . . . and should it happen that a person chosen for such an office were deposed for abuse of trust, he would then be exactly what he was before."[12]

In contrast to the medieval practice of appointing bishops and priests to their offices without the consent of the people they were charged to serve, Luther was advocating what he knew to be the practice in the early church: the popular election of leaders. "In times gone by Christians used to choose their bishops and priests in this way from among their own number."[13] To say the least, this was a novel if not alarming reform: transferring power from the hierarchy into the hands of the community itself.[14] In effect this reversal of medieval practice shifted attention from episcopal leadership to the baptized assembly and its pastoral leaders.[15] The community of "priests" (Latin, *sacerdotes*) received the authority, as an assembly guided by the Spirit, to select and to dismiss its own leaders (Latin, *ministri*) who acted on its behalf. "When a bishop consecrates it is nothing else than that in the place and stead of the whole community, *all of whom have like power*, he takes a person and charges [that person] to exercise this power on behalf of others."[16] Luther would argue for the absolute necessity of an ordained ministry, an "office," yet one that only serves the word and the sacraments at the behest of the community. Thus, those persons chosen from among the members of the Christian assembly as leaders would not join a permanent hierarchy ruling over the assembly (as sanctioned by canon law) but would serve as public ministers within the assembly.

While he would never stray from his teaching on human passivity before "alien" righteousness or justifying grace, Luther's address also brought to awareness the active and participatory dimension of the Christian assembly. Indeed, the pressing need to "start something" or "start the game" was the urgent thread that ran throughout the entire letter. One was consecrated an active "priest" in the Christian community. Christians should choose their own priests and bishops. Christians should forthrightly serve the community with their skills or talents. The power to forgive has been given to the entire community, not Peter and his successors alone.[17] The power to "test and judge what is right or wrong in matters of faith" is the possession of all Christians.[18] The Scriptures are to be the commonly held treasure of the Christian assembly.[19] Such an emphasis on the active and conscious participation of Christians in their common life would lead Luther to translate the Bible into German, preach and teach in German, translate and write hymns for the assembly to sing (in contrast to the medieval practice of hiring professionals to sing during the Mass), and institute reforms in the Mass that, among other things, would encourage greater congregational participation. This call to active participation by the "priesthood of the baptized," rooted in the memory of the early New Testament

Figure 4.3. *The pope is mocked by a peasant,* 1527, from a work on the end of the world by the reformer Andreas Osiander.

communities, captured both the growing anticlericalism of the age and what Peter Matheson calls the desire for a "recasting of the whole of social and political, as well as ecclesiastical, reality."[20] While Luther's reform project was rooted in theology, in the proper understanding of God and the relationship between God and humanity as reflected in the Bible, his call to reform, rooted in that theology, was beginning to spill outward in ecclesial and social reform.

The Worldly Trajectory of Baptism

Luther's criticism of a society divided into spiritual and secular spheres was rooted in his understanding of the New Testament and the sacrament of baptism. Indeed, he used the plain sense of Scripture (e.g., "You are a royal priesthood and priestly realm") to cut through what he believed were the many theological, philosophical, and legal obstructions that had clogged the "spring" of the gospel and its sacraments during the previous three hundred years: "Through canon law the Romanists have almost destroyed and made unknown the wondrous grace and authority of baptism and justification."[21] At the same time he used the central teaching on justification by grace to interpret anew the sacrament of baptism. In his mind no longer could baptismal consecration be viewed as the beginning of a lifetime project to prepare as best one could for the last judgment, to cooperate with the grace of Christ by doing or believing that which would secure a merciful judgment and everlasting life. Rather, baptism promised the forgiveness of sin throughout life, grafted one into the living Christ, and initiated one into the priesthood of all the baptized. The trajectory of baptismal consecration effectively shifted the baptized from concern about the "the life of the world to come" to his or her presence in this world.

By insisting that virtually all baptized Christians participated in the "spiritual" estate, Luther denied the "superior" status of monastic or priestly work and affirmed the everyday work of all Christians, that work which was undertaken in the world.

> Just as those who are now called "spiritual," that is, priests, bishops, or popes, are neither different from other Christians nor superior to them, except that they are charged with the administration of the

word of God and the sacraments, which is their work and office, so it is with the temporal authorities. They bear the sword and rod in their hand to punish the wicked and protect the good. A cobbler, a smith, a peasant—each has the work and office of his trade, and yet they are all alike consecrated priests and bishops. Further, everyone must benefit and serve every other by means of his own work or office so that in this way many kinds of work may be done for the bodily and spiritual welfare of the community, just as all the members of the body serve one another [1 Cor. 12:14–26].[22]

The notion that the "ordinary" work of daily life, the work of a baptized cobbler or peasant, could hold theological or spiritual value signaled a reinterpretation of the term *vocation* (Latin, *vocatio*; German, *Beruf*). In Roman Catholic circles "vocation" or "calling" had been and would be used in reference to the ordained ministry or the religious life; one could receive a "vocation" to the priesthood but not to the fire station or the textile mill. Luther and his colleagues would apply "vocation" to the ordinary work of every Christian "done for the bodily and spiritual welfare of the community." That work, of course, would be accomplished within "the world," within the economic, political, and social fabric of one's society. While Luther continually emphasized the movement of God toward humanity in the incarnation, justification, and baptism, one begins to see in his teaching on the priesthood of the baptized, a corollary to his teaching on "proper" or "social righteousness": the baptized Christian is to recognize his or her work as a service to the neighbor, a work that possesses both "theological" and "worldly" value. Rather than bringing one into a *private* relationship with God—soul drawn into Soul—baptism consecrated the infant or the adult to a life of faith made active in *public* service, in service to the common good: the good of other citizens in the political community, the good of family members in the domestic community, the good of other Christians in the ecclesial community. For Luther such public service was rooted in and guided by theology.

In continuity with Jewish and Christian claims, Luther suggested that God cannot be seen, heard, or touched directly by creatures in the manner that humans see, hear, or touch each other. While God may have conversed with the primal ancestors, whispered to the patriarch

Abraham, revealed the divine presence in a burning bush, or led the Hebrews out of slavery with a pillar of fire, God remains absolute mystery, an ineffable mystery whose thoughts and intentions cannot be known or penetrated by creatures possessed of limited ability and knowledge. The transcendent God is as distant from humans as heaven is from hell: "From this absolute God everyone should flee who does not want to perish, because human nature and the absolute God—for the sake of teaching we use this familiar term—are the bitterest of enemies. Human weakness cannot help being crushed by such majesty, as Scripture reminds us over and over."[23] And yet, Luther maintained, the "absolute" God offers continual care for the cosmos, the planet, and all creatures. Indeed, Luther would write, nine years later, in his commentary on the first article of the Apostles' Creed, that

> [God] makes all creation help provide the benefits and necessities of life—sun, moon, and stars in the heavens; day and night; air, fire, water, the earth and all that it yields and brings forth; birds, fish, animals, grain and all sorts of produce. Moreover, he gives all physical and temporal blessings—good government, peace, security . . . everything in heaven and on earth besides, is daily given, sustained, and protected by God.[24]

While God remains inaccessible and ineffable mystery, God is continually serving the creation in a *hidden* manner through the earthly elements God creates: night and day, water and fire, soil and air, the

Figure 4.4. Jean Crespin, *God creates all things,* 1527, from an early 16th c. edition of the Bible.

human community. These are the fundamental elements from which and through which all creatures are sustained in life. This continual public service to the creation is accomplished daily "out of pure love and goodness, without our merit." Here Luther affirms the teaching on justification and his insistence that God is continually coming to or advancing toward creation with "boundless love," as an inexhaustible fountain of life. The absolute God, God beyond any human words or images, is revealed through the works of creation, that is, if humans can perceive the extraordinary in the ordinary.

Indeed, the ineffable God of majesty and power—which no human eye can behold and live—is "clothed," as it were, in what humans may consider the ordinary, mundane, or earthy. Luther could thus affirm the medieval principle of *finitum capax infinitum*—the finite is capable of holding and revealing the infinite: God speaks a Word that becomes incarnate in Jesus of Nazareth, what for Luther was God's ultimate speaking. In Jesus of Nazareth "the Word of life and light" (John 1:1-5) is revealed in human form.

While Luther spoke of the Word of God being "clothed" in humanity, he also used the term *mask* (German, *Maske*) to describe the immanence, public presence, and gifts of God among and for God's creatures:

> What else is all our work to God—whether in the fields, in the garden, in the city, in the house, in war, or in government—but . . . a child's performance, by which he wants to give his gifts in the fields, at home, and everywhere else? These are the masks of God behind which he wants to remain concealed and do all things. . . . [God] could give children without using men and women but does not want to do this. Instead, he joins man and woman so that it appears to be the work of man and woman, and yet he does it under the cover of such masks.[25]

While the mystery of God can never be fully grasped by humans, God nonetheless reveals God's continual sustenance of the creation through the masks of fertile field, sexual union, secure home, and just government—to name but a few of the means through which creation experiences the providence of the Creator. Arrayed before human beings enlightened by faith, then, are the many means through which God "has given to us himself with all creation and has abundantly provided for us in this life, apart from the fact that he has also showered us with inexpressible eternal blessings through his Son and the Holy Spirit."[26]

At the same time Luther would speak of the sacraments as masks of God:

Pastors are nothing but channels through which Christ leads and transmits his Gospel from the Father to us. Therefore, wherever you hear the Gospel properly taught or see a person baptized, wherever you see someone administer or receive the Sacrament, or wherever you witness someone absolving another, there you may say without hesitation: "Today I beheld God's Word and work. Yes, I saw and heard God Himself preaching and baptizing." To be sure, the tongue, the voice, the hands, etc., are those of a human being; but the Word and the ministry are really those of the Divine Majesty. Hence it must be viewed and believed as though God's own voice were resounding from heaven and as though we were seeing him administering Baptism or the Sacrament with His own hands.... When we get to heaven, we shall see God differently; then no clouds and no darkness will obscure our view. But here on earth we shall not perceive him with our senses and our thoughts. No, here we see [God], as St. Paul states (1 Cor. 13:12), "in a mirror dimly," enveloped in an image, namely, in the Word and the sacraments. These are his masks or garments.[27]

That the sacrament of baptism was celebrated with the earthly element of water, wedded to the promise spoken by Christ, underscored Luther's assertion that God conforms God's presence to human capacity in order to serve human need. Human word and earthly element are set forth as active signs or masks of God: they communicate God's presence and intentions publicly, in the midst of an assembly of Christians, citizens of both realm and household. While some Christians metaphorically "ascend into the clouds" and are concerned about what God thinks and does "up there," Luther wrote, such speculation is illusory and thus fruitless, an activity that actually leads these Christians to think they know the capacious mind of God when, in fact, they know nothing but their own small thoughts. "We do not separate or differentiate between God and his Word or ministry, given to us through Christ; nor do we seek God in another way or view [God] in a different light." The ineffable mystery of God is revealed to and conformed to human capacity: "When God reveals himself to us, it is necessary for [God] to do so through a veil or wrapper and to say: 'Look! Under this wrapper you will be sure to take hold of me.' "[28]

Yet if water and the gifts of nature can be interpreted as masks of God's continual and providential care for all creation, and if the sacrament of baptism—celebrated with water and promise—can be understood as a living sign or mask of salvific work among humans, then it should not be surprising to find Luther speaking of the baptized themselves as masks of God's advance into public life.

> [One] should regard all [human labor] as being the work of our Lord God under a mask, as it were, beneath which he himself alone effects and accomplishes what we desire. He commands us to equip ourselves for this reason also, that he might conceal his own work under this disguise, and allow those who boast to go their way, and strengthen those who are worried, so that men [and women] will not tempt him. . . . Indeed, one could very well say that the course of the world, and especially the doing of his saints, are God's mask, under which he conceals himself and so marvelously exercises dominion.[29]

Marrying, raising children, bathing a person, conversing with others, sharing a meal, governing the state, defending the weak, or tilling the fields may appear to the unenlightened as merely ordinary things—all elements in the cycle of life, things to be done out of custom or need. Yet for the baptized Christian enlightened by the Spirit, Luther argued, these activities or relationships are natural means of grace through which God works in a particular time and place.[30] Indeed, the baptized Christian is sacramentally consecrated as a mask of God and agent of grace in the world, extending the advance of God's rule into the economic, political, and social dimensions of life lived on this earth. Thus, by working, a farmer participates in the growth of the fruits of the field. But this is no mundane activity devoid of meaning and purpose: cultivation of fields that will bring forth stores of food is a mask of God's providential care of hungry human beings. Only the force of original sin blinds humans to the profound significance of "ordinary" human work or the cycles and seasons of nature as the *opus Dei*, the work of God. Indeed, Luther would argue that growing crops to feed the hungry is something just as great as [Jesus'] multiplication of the loaves and fish in the wilderness.[31]

Figure 4.5. *The Parable of the laborers in the vineyard,* 1540, from one of Luther's commentaries on the epistles and gospels appointed for Advent.

Consequently, when parents care for each other and their children, when judges and magistrates rule justly, when physicians tend to the sick, when grocers provide food stuffs at a fair price, when priests or pastors faithfully minister among the homebound or dying as well as the able and healthy, when teachers tend to the needs of their students, they are "using their gifts to the glory of God and for the common good."[32] By symbolically destroying the two estates of late medieval Christianity, Luther began the process of dismantling the hierarchical order of the Western church, an order that had been in place close to a thousand years. In his insistence that an ecclesiology of Christian egalitarianism flow from the sacrament of baptism, he shifted the late medieval perception of public ministry from its ontological moorings to a functionalist center. But, perhaps most important, by drawing attention to the baptized Christian as a sacrament and mask of God's work in the world, in the economic, political, and social fabric of life, a new valorization of "ordinary work" began to emerge in his thought and in the imagination of those Germans drawn so quickly and ardently to his reform project. The "world" had been tipped upside down, as it were. Who could have imagined that the daily labor of a cleaning woman, a farmer, or a lawyer could be as valuable, as "sacramental," as holy as the ministrations of a nun, a priest, or a bishop? Who would have thought that the translation of a Mediterranean text in the language of the people would allow ancient words of reform to be placed on the lips of peasants? Who would have thought that the way forward into the future was by returning to the past and to the font?

DEVELOPMENTS

5

Consider the Broad Fields

The Biblical Invitation to Feed the Hungry

Martin Luther was ordained to the priesthood on February 27, 1507, in the cathedral church of Erfurt, Germany. Within a few weeks he began his study of theology at the University of Erfurt but was assigned within a year to the Augustinian cloister in Wittenberg. There he both continued his theological studies and gave a series of lectures on moral philosophy at the town's new university. In the spring of 1509, he received a bachelor's degree in biblical studies and, in 1511, a doctorate in theology from the University of Wittenberg.

By 1512 Luther had been appointed professor of Bible. He began his academic career as a Scripture scholar by lecturing on the biblical books, a work that he would continue for the remainder of his life. Coupled with his responsibilities in the university, Luther was appointed to the pastoral administration of the parish church, St. Marien, where he preached on the biblical texts assigned in the medieval lectionary for each Sunday and festival day of the year. Luther encountered the Bible as both a preacher charged with the pastoral formation of the congregation and as a scholar responsible for his students' academic study of Scripture. From the winter of 1513 until the spring or summer of 1515, he lectured on the Psalms. From 1515 through 1518 he lectured on the letters of Paul to the Romans and the Galatians and then the Letter to the Hebrews. In the winter of 1518–19, he began a second course of lectures on the Psalms. From December 1522 to the end of February 1523, a period of eleven weeks that coincided with his protective custody at the Wartburg Castle after having been excommunicated and declared a criminal in the empire, he translated the entire New Testament into German.

To say the least, Luther's imagination, theology, preaching, and social initiatives were immersed in and shaped by the biblical text. Indeed, when Hans Sachs portrayed Luther in 1523 as the "Wittenberg nightingale" singing to the rising dawn, his metaphorical depiction of the reformer as a songbird was inspired by a biblical text: the gospel narration of Jesus' entry into Jerusalem (Luke 19:29-40), a text inscribed at the base of his drawing. When, in the story, a group of Pharisees told Jesus to make his disciples stop shouting out the good news of his arrival in Jerusalem, he responded, "I tell you, if these [disciples] were silent, the very stones would shout out" [v. 40]. For Sachs, Luther was the nightingale that would not stop "shouting" or "singing" Scripture, the "new" song of reform.

In this regard Luther was not alone. The many reformers of church and society in western Europe were deeply influenced by their humanist colleagues who pointed to the classical inheritance of antiquity and encouraged a return *ad fontes*, to the springs of fresh and pure teaching that flowed from the ancient past. When Luther and his reforming colleagues looked to the past, however, their eyes did not fall on the

Figure 5.1. Lucas Cranach the Younger, *The vineyard of the Lord*, 1569, in the Wittenberg City Church St. Marien; fresh water flows from the well into the field Luther is cultivating. Photo © SuperStock, Inc. / SuperStock.

works of Plato and Aristotle or Cicero and Seneca but the biblical text and the writings of the Greek and Latin bishops, the "doctors of the church," who were among the first Christian commentators on the Bible. Luther, Sachs seemed to say, was singing the Bible and singing it in a language that Germans could understand. Yet Luther's appeal was not to an ancient text that was simply superior to what the late medieval scholastics had taught. Rather, for Luther, the Word of God was first of all the living voice and presence of the risen Christ speaking and acting in Luther's own age, through the medium of human speech, a living presence to which the written text—the Bible—was a sure and authoritative witness.[1]

Convinced that he lived in a religious system marked by corruption, Luther had come to recognize by 1518, if not before, that the authentic springs of Christian teaching had been successively clogged, obscured, and polluted by a tangle of almost impenetrable branches that had grown steadfastly since the twelfth and thirteenth centuries: "I plainly believe that reform of the church is only possible through the total uprooting and replacement of the canons and papal decretals, and of scholastic theology, philosophy, and logic as they are now taught. My convictions on this have developed to the point that I beg the Lord each day that as soon as possible the pure study of the Bible and the Fathers of the Church might be reestablished."[2] To engage in the process of reform, then, was to pull away the overgrown branches of papal control, canon law, and church custom, to pick up and cast aside the rocks of churchly abuses, to uproot and burn what he considered the pernicious weeds of late medieval teaching that had obscured access to the spring of God's own freely flowing life. Indeed, Lucas Cranach the Younger would paint the Lutheran reformers cultivating a growing vineyard where fresh water was being poured from a sturdy German font, an epitaph image found in the Wittenberg city church of St. Marien. To clear away what he believed was the accumulated bracken of the previous three hundred years, Luther found in Scripture what he considered its central axes and teachings—the Pauline description of justification by grace, the Christ who embraces humanity's suffering, and the living faith that supplants superstition and legalism. With these central symbols—*sola scriptura, sola gratia, solus Christus,* and *sola fide*—Luther found the clippers, the shovel, and the hoe that would continue to reveal "the pure spring of the Gospel."

Christ as *Donum* and *Exemplum*

In 1519 Luther preached on the distinction between "alien righteousness" and "proper righteousness," the former received passively "from without" through baptism as the justification of the sinner, the latter issuing forth as its active social expression in service to the neighbor in need.[3] Following that dialectical pattern Luther wrote an instruction on how to interpret the Bible using the central teaching on justification by grace through faith. That work, "A Brief Instruction on What to Look for and Expect in the Gospels," was written in 1522 while he was translating the Bible during his exile at the Wartburg Castle.

In this instruction Luther argued that the many biblical writers described or announced only one gospel. That "gospel" was nothing less than "a discourse about Christ, that he is the Son of God and became [human] for us, that he died and was raised, that he has been established as Lord over all things. . . . This is the gospel in a nutshell."[4] As there is only one Christ, he wrote, there can be only one gospel. Yet that "discourse" or story about Christ, "God's and David's Son," is found not only in the four canonical Gospels but throughout the entire sweep of Scripture, in the writings of the Hebrew prophets, the letters of the early Christian writers, and the Revelation of John. Thus, Luther could recognize "pure gospel" in Isaiah's depiction of the suffering servant since the poem speaks of "how Christ should die for us and bear our sins." Luther's insistence that the Word of God and the sacraments of the Word be interpreted as *pro nobis*, "for us," as the announcement of forgiveness and salvation, was rooted in his teaching on justification by grace: in baptism God acts decisively in favor of persons turned inward, apart from any meritorious actions or beliefs that might appear to make them "worthy" of God's favor. In the instruction Luther correlated the teaching on justification by grace with his understanding of the gospel:

> The chief article and foundation of the gospel is that . . . you accept and recognize [Christ] as a gift, as a present that God has given

you and that is your own. This means that when you see or hear of Christ doing or suffering something, you do not doubt that Christ himself, with his deeds and suffering, belongs to you. On this you may depend as surely as if you had done it yourself; indeed as if you were Christ himself. See, this is what it means to have a proper grasp of the gospel, that is, of the overwhelming goodness of God. . . . This is the great fire of the love of God for us, whereby the heart and conscience become happy, secure, and content. This is what preaching the Christian faith means.[5]

The first thing any Christian reader, student, theologian, or preacher of Scripture must grasp is Christ as the *donum Dei*, the gift of God, "given you for your very own." The living Christ, who dwells with the baptized Christian, nourishes faith in the inner person and makes one Christian. That is, the "overwhelming goodness" and the "great fire of the love of God for us" are not mere "values" or spiritualized abstractions but have a visible form in the historical Jesus and a continuing presence in the many baptized, animated by the Spirit, who form his "body" in the world.

Of course every affirmation can possess an implicit denial. In the instruction Luther was intent on correcting what he considered two egregious errors in late medieval theology and preaching: the interpretation of the Gospels and the Epistles as books of law that must be followed to secure one's salvation and the transformation of Christ into "a Moses" who teaches legal precepts or presents himself as an "example" for Christians to imitate. While the leaders of the *devotio moderna* advised Christians to imitate the simplicity of Christ and find the humble, ordinary Christ in the Gospels, Luther would not accept this *imitatio Christi* as the first impulse in reading Scripture or understanding the life of the baptized. While he acknowledged that the New Testament does present Christ as an example (1 Peter 2:21), this should not be the first way to "grasp" him.

When you see how [Christ] prays, fasts, helps people, and shows them love, so also you should do, both for yourself and for your neighbor. However, this is the smallest part of the gospel, on the basis of which it cannot yet even be called gospel. For on this level Christ is of no more help to you than some other saint. His life remains his own and does not as yet contribute anything to you. In short this mode [of understanding Christ as simply an example] does not make Christians but only hypocrites.[6]

In effect Luther was arguing that this late medieval emphasis on imitating Christ would lead the Christian to imagine that his or her "imitation"—helping people and showing them love as Christ did—was the primary mark of Christian identity. Luther groaned at this well-intentioned advice but also diagnosed its problem: while it may be good if not necessary, there is nothing distinctively Christian about helping people. In the same way that "proper" or social righteousness does not make one Christian, so searching Scripture for the "example of Christ" in order to imitate that example in one's life does not make one Christian. Only God makes one Christian through the act of justification, the reception of "alien" righteousness, mediated in baptism; only the living, indwelling Christ makes one a Christian, that Christ who is first received as *donum*, as gift. Yet Luther did not abolish the *imitatio Christi*.

> Now when you have Christ as the foundation and chief blessing of your salvation, then the other part follows: that you take him as your example, giving yourself in service to your neighbor just as you see that Christ has given himself for you. See, there faith and love move forward, God's commandment is fulfilled, and a person is happy and fearless to do and to suffer all things. Therefore make note of this, that Christ as a gift nourishes your faith and makes you a Christian. But Christ as an example exercises your works. These do not make you a Christian. Actually they come forth from you because you have already been made a Christian. As widely as a gift differs from an example, so widely does faith differ from works, for faith possesses nothing of its own, only the deeds and life of Christ. Works have something of your own in them, yet they should not belong to you but to your neighbor.[7]

As "proper" or "social" righteousness flows from its "alien" source, so imitating Christ the *exemplum* flows from receiving him as *donum*.[8]

The preaching of the gospel, Luther claimed, is nothing less than Christ coming to the listeners and "offering the soul . . . help and favor through the gospel." The function of Christ's example—his praying, fasting, helping people, and showing love—is to benefit the Christian in his relationship with his or her neighbor in need. The practice of the imitation of Christ is always, in Luther's thought, bent toward the other. "It is necessary that you . . . deal with your neighbor in the very same way [as Christ has dealt with you], be given also to [the neighbor] as a gift and an example."[9] The Christian is taught by Christ, albeit in a "loving and friendly way," what to do in the world. Passive in the reception of Christ as gift, the Christian is to become active in service to the neighbor in need because such work fulfills the commands of Christ, actually benefits the neighbor, and tests the authenticity of faith, that gift itself that rules and guides one's living in the world with other persons.

At the conclusion of his instruction, Luther wrote that "it is ultimately true that the gospel itself is our guide and instructor in the Scriptures."[10] For Luther that gospel first presented Christ the *donum* and then the *exemplum*, effectively recasting the entire sweep of Scripture as a book that promises grace and denounces injustice, comforts the poor and terrifies the haughty, fills the hungry with good things and sends the rich away empty-handed. That the Creator of the universe would be revealed in the lowly figure of Christ as "free gift" would not be lost on the priest and professor who was quick to give away his food to the hungry poor who begged at his door.[11]

Luther's Interpretation of Scripture

As a young theology student, Luther was trained in the four lively methods of biblical exegesis that had gained increasing popularity in medieval universities since their articulation by John Cassian in the fifth century: the literal or historical sense of Scripture, the allegorical or christological sense, the tropological or moral sense, and the anagogical or eschatological sense. To demonstrate how the fourfold understanding could illuminate and interpret the biblical text, Cassian applied each sense to the term *Jerusalem*. In the literal or historical sense, Jerusalem refers to the city built on a mountain range in the land of Israel; in the christological sense, it refers to the church of Christ, the community or "city" of the baptized; in the moral sense, it refers to the human soul, the "inner city," and its capacity for vice and virtue; and in the eschatological sense, it could be interpreted as the "holy city, the new Jerusalem, coming down out of heaven from God" (Rev. 21:2).[12] While the first "sense" of Scripture was never lost in medieval exegesis, the more-than-literal senses had become dominant as Christian monastic mysticism flourished, as medieval preachers attempted to communicate the moral claims of the Bible to their listeners, and as concern for the future and one's eternal destiny focused on the "last things" and the day of judgment.[13] Without completely dismissing allegory—it was present in the New Testament, Luther noted—he had begun, by the early 1520s, to focus his interpretation on a literal or, what he preferred to call, a historical sense and a spiritual or christological sense of Scripture.

What had become central for Luther in his interpretation of the Scriptures was clear in his instruction of 1522 ("All Scripture tends toward [Christ]"[14]) yet present already in a sermon he preached on the anniversary of his baptism in 1515: "Whoever wants to read the Bible must make sure he is not wrong, for the Scriptures can be easily stretched and guided, but no one should guide them according to his emotions; he should lead them to the well, that is to the cross of Christ, then he will certainly be right and cannot fail."[15] With this christological center Luther could "find" Christ in the writings of the Old Testament just as he could in the New and, thus, admit of a spiritual sense of Scripture that was christological. Influenced by humanist scholarship as well as his focus on the humanity and suffering of Christ, he promoted the literal, historical, or "plain" sense of Scripture. Thus, Luther would recognize Christ, the Word of God, speaking in and through the psalms of David[16] (i.e., the spiritual sense[17]) and Christ quoting a psalm of David as he was dying on the cross—"My God, my God, why have you forsaken me?"[18] (i.e., the historical or plain sense). Both senses were alive in his interpretation of Scripture. Consequently, he understood "bread" in the fourth petition of the Lord's Prayer ("Give us this day our daily bread") as a reference to the Word or God or the consecrated bread of the Mass (a spiritual sense) as well as the loaves of bread prepared in a bakery and eaten daily by his fellow Germans (a historical or plain sense).[19] Indeed, when Luther spoke about feeding the hungry, he employed both senses of Scripture.

The Spiritual Sense of Feeding the Hungry

Luther was not alone when he allowed the figures, events, and say-ings of the Bible to judge his own time, the ancient word pronouncing mercy or condemnation on the tumultuous world in which he lived. As Peter Matheson notes:

> The Reformers did not dredge Scripture for proof-texts. The Bible's light and clarity were not so much a doctrinal source or a blueprint for structural change. Rather, when we read their sermons . . . we find biblical personalities and images swimming up to the surface of their minds. An irruption, explosion, eruption of the biblical imagination of the patriarchs, prophets, psalmists, and apostles took place. . . . They learnt [sic] to sink themselves, heart and mind, into the tonality of the biblical world. They thought deeply about the way in which biblical concerns had to be accommodated to radically different situations.[20]

Drawing on the image of agricultural and human devastation as recorded in the book of Genesis,[21] Luther spoke of a famine gripping the land, indeed, all of Christianity. Yet this was not a physical but a spiritual famine, a "famine" of the Word of God without which women and men would starve and perish. "Since we abandoned [God's] Scrip-tures, it is not surprising that he has abandoned us to the teaching of the pope and to the lies of men."[22] In the harshest terms Luther portrayed this spiritual famine and its consequences: "Who would not prefer physical afflictions like pestilence, famine, or the sword to a fam-ine of the Word, which is always coupled with eternal damnation?"[23] Where there is no nourishment with the Word of God, the soul, the inner person, hungers and eventually dies. When faith, the vital force of life and freedom within the inner person, receives no spiritual food or drink, one's capacity to trust God and serve the neighbor in love is thwarted. "If [the soul] has the Word of God it is rich and lacks noth-ing since it is the Word of life, truth, light, peace, righteousness, salva-tion, joy, liberty, wisdom, power, grace, glory, and of every incalculable blessing. . . . On the other hand, there is no more terrible disaster with which the wrath of God can afflict men than a famine of the hearing of his Word."[24] The Word of God is, nonetheless, not just any word of Scripture. Rather, the Word of God is Christ himself speaking the promises and grace of God in contrast to the mandates of God and the law. Ruled by faith, the Christian hungers for this Word: "Christ wanted to avert our harm and doom by . . . exhorting us to turn our attention to the eternal food, for this food does not perish. How eagerly you should strive for this food and not despise it but esteem it above everything as an enduring food that gives eternal life."[25] One is to seek out this Word and allow nothing else to serve as a substitute for its life-giving nourishment.[26] As Luther would write in his hymn to Christian hope, "Your people's pasture is your Word, their souls to feed and nourish."[27] In this metaphorical pasture food and drink are given freely; one can neither earn nor pay for them. This feeding of "hungry souls," nonetheless, is a mediated feeding, what Luther and his colleagues would come to call the "means of grace," the public proclamation, singing, and sermonic interpretation of Scripture and the public celebration of the scriptural sacraments of baptism and the Lord's Supper. Luther was not averse to complaining loudly that the Word had been silenced for centuries and the Mass had been turned into a superstitious "work" and a "profit-making business"[28] sold and traded to those who could afford the fee. In contrast Christ declares that "he himself is an excellent baker, and offers to provide what field and purse cannot supply."[29]

Figure 5.2. Leonard Parasol, *The hand of God throws seed on the field*, 1595, a printer's device in the Roman Pontifical of Clement VIII.

Luther would never depart from this "spiritual" interpretation of Scripture. Where Christ is present with his Word, there is spiritual food and drink to nourish the faith of the "inner" person, that faith which directs the "outer" person in his or her relationships with others in this world. Yet Luther also recognized quite clearly that Christ was already present in the world, present "in his needy ones," in a world marked by misfortune, sorrow, and the unjust suffering of the innocent.[30] In this world the "ungodly" as well as the "godly" suffer with natural disaster and, more insidiously, from the depredations of other human beings. This recognition of physical need was nothing new to Luther or his contemporaries; it was, sadly and tragically, the black thread that snaked through the fabric of early modern Europe. Indeed, in the *Spiegel* of Scripture, one could recognize Lazarus in Germany's hungry women and men begging food from the rich who "feasted sumptuously every day" (Luke 16:19). One could see this as well in Scripture: a great and hungry crowd gathered around Christ who blessed God for bread, broke it and shared it, with enough left over (Mark 6:30-44). And this: a group of Christians gathering a collection for those who suffered with hunger and famine (1 Cor. 11:21, 33).

The Historical Sense of Feeding the Hungry

As a young biblical student and monk, Luther had followed a scrupulously ascetic regimen,[31] one that included fasting, physical mortification, and disdain for the ordinary needs and pleasures of life. Without asserting a causal relationship, it would seem, nonetheless, that his early interpretation of Scripture corresponded in some ways with his ascetic dedication. For instance, in his commentary on Psalm 104,[32] part of his early lectures on the Psalms (1513–15), Luther admitted of God's providence in providing creatures with physical nourishment (the plain sense of the text). Yet he quickly elaborated on the spiritual significance of the text, suggesting that the verse "When you open your hand, they are filled with good things" (v. 28) should be interpreted as God "feeding" the creation with and through the preaching and teaching of the Word: "Wisdom plays this whole game mystically in the church, for He feeds all the creatures of God without the work of men, and when He gives and opens His hand they gather and are filled with good, which is the Word of the Gospel. For who but Christ has opened the Gospel? And so, behold, he expresses the same thing by means of many symbols."[33]

Luther would not depart from interpreting Scripture in a spiritual sense, yet his appreciation for the plain or historical sense would continue to grow throughout the early 1520s and beyond as he responded to requests for advice concerning the economic, political, and social concerns of his day. Indeed, one ought not to exclude the influence of his biography on his theology. His departure from and published criticism of monastic life, his entrance into marriage and the subsequent birth of children, and his encounter with the hungry poor at his door or on the streets of Wittenberg helped him participate in the Reformation's "wide recovery of the earthy humanity of Scripture."[34] As a biblical scholar whose imagination was shaped by the study of Scripture and as a theologian engaged in the pressing crises of the early sixteenth century,[35] Luther allowed the biblical text to interpret the questions and controversies of his day.

On the one hand, Luther was acutely sensitive to the powerful role of self-preservation in human thought and action, an aggressive self-centered focus that could obscure too readily the neighbor's need and one's dependence on the Creator. At the same time, he also grew in his "appreciation for the goodness of God's creation"[36] and the appropriate use of God's natural gifts in the social order. "Luther's discovery of the world as a given, promised domain extricates him from a monastic denial of life and corresponding flight from the world. As a reformer living entirely out of joy in creation, he discovers worldliness as a theological category."[37] This "appreciation" of creation in its plain or earthy or "worldly" sense became clearer in his explanations of the first article of the Apostles' Creed ("I believe in God, the Father Almighty, Creator of heaven and earth")[38] and the fourth petition of the Lord's Prayer ("Give us today our daily bread"),[39] first preached in a series of catechetical sermons in the summer of 1528 and then revised for publication as the German Catechism or Large Catechism in the fall of 1528. There one can recognize the theological implication embedded in the teaching on justification by grace: the movement of God toward, into, and through this creation: "You see, God wishes to show us how he cares for us in all our needs and faithfully provides for our daily sustenance. Although he gives and provides these blessings bountifully, even to the godless and rogues, yet he wishes us to ask for them so that we may realize that we have received them from his hand and may recognize in them his fatherly goodness toward us."[40]

God Feeds All Creation

Luther stood within one stream of Christian theology when he claimed that the Creator feeds not only human beings but all creatures. While there are moments in his writing when he reflected a singularly andro-centric view of creation ("God daily and abundantly provides . . . all the necessities and nourishment for this body and life,"[41] and"[God] makes all creation help provide the benefits and necessities of life"[42]), he also clearly affirmed that God is not only interested in feeding people but other creatures as well. For instance, when he commented on the provision of herbs and fruits in the ark (Gen. 6:21), he noted that "[God] is looking out for the human being and for the other animals, that they may be preserved and that through their preservation the species may be preserved. . . . Through God's providence [the animals] also had food suited to their nature."[43] The implication of this affirmation of divine nourishment for all creation is quickly focused on its social implication: God demands that humans do not waste the gifts of creation but use them wisely and with thanksgiving. As God has carefully chosen what will nourish life, so humans are to care for that which they have received as divine gift. "It would be a sin," he warned, "to expect food from heaven when one is hungry and not provide for it in some other manner or ask for it."[44] Noah was not ordered to wait in the ark for the miraculous appearance of food, Luther noted, but was told to employ normal means for gathering food. In a similar manner he pointed out that Christ commanded the apostles to eat what was set before them, to use natural means of nourishment.

Figure 5.3. *God and creation*, 1530, from one of Luther's commentaries on the epistles and gospels appointed for Advent.

While Luther understood the Bible as a historical narrative that revealed a salvific purpose focused in Jesus of Nazareth, "the son of

David and the son of God," he also recognized that the events of the past, narrated in the Bible, were vividly alive in his own day, in the present. It is a theological affirmation that may be difficult for the modern reader to grasp, especially in a world where religious or theological claims rest on the margins of a secular worldview and in religious contexts where the social, economic, or political dimensions of Scripture are muted. For Luther, however, neither was the case. Since the Word of God, the agent of creation (John 1:1-3) and salvation (John 1:29), could not be bound to a text, to the past, or to an individual's disembodied soul, but is ever present in the world,[45] the Word of God is *continually* creating and saving the world: "God remains with his creation, is effective in it, continually allows new animals and human beings to be born, and continually grants new beginnings and in this way preserves creation. God's *conservatio*, God's sustaining of creation, is, to be sure, a sign of his abiding goodness as the creator."[46] While Luther could affirm that God provided food and drink for all hungry creatures "in the beginning," that provisioning and subsequent conserving of creatures continues *in the present* through "natural means." All existence, in this regard, is a mediated existence dependent on God and others. The Creator does not act theoretically but actually through creatures: the infant is utterly dependent for life on the milk that comes from her or his mother. The milk itself nourishes life and is the very means through which "God with his living Word" continues to feed the weak and the hungry. "God makes use of . . . the service of nature and of natural means."[47]

Provision of Food and Drink Always Intended by God

Origen of Alexandria, the early third-century biblical scholar and friend of Neoplatonism, would claim that the two creation stories in Genesis actually reflect two separate creations: the first one a "spiritual" and incorporeal creation due to grace, the second a bodily and material creation due to sin. In a Christianized Neoplatonism, spiritual or intellectual life was and is considered superior to material and earthly life; indeed, the latter was perceived as a punishment for sin. While the notion of a "double creation" never gained wide currency in Christian theology,[48] the claim that matter was inherently inferior to spirit or

mind—a "fall" from God's original intention—gained a steady following in subsequent centuries. Thus, it was possible to argue that the need
to nourish the body was, at worse, due to human sin. At best, concern
with bodily need was a transitory temptation, one that hindered dedication to truly "spiritual" matters. As we have noted the young Luther
practiced ascetic control over the body and its needs, a practice engen-
dered under the influence of an ascetic discipline that could easily deni-
grate the body and its needs. Yet the older Luther was clear that God
intended to provide the first humans with food and drink from the very
moment of their creation. Eating and drinking to satisfy hunger could
not be associated with sin: "Here you see how solicitous God is for the
man he has created. First he created the earth like a house in which he
should live. Then he arranged the other things he regarded as necessary
for life. Finally, he gave the gift of procreation to the man he created.
Now he also provides his food that nothing may be lacking for leading
his life in the easiest possible manner."[49]

Since Paradise was created as a distinctive "culture," the Creator
placed herbs and fruit-bearing trees there, "delightful to behold and
pleasant to use." The meaning
of God's declaration—"I have
given you every plant yielding
seed ... and every tree with
seed in its fruit" (Gen. 1:29)—is
this: food was necessary from
the very beginning. Hunger was
not a result of disobedience to
God. The experience of hunger and thirst was and is inherent in the human condition
and its fundamental goodness
in Paradise. Indeed, Luther saw
the teaching on justification by
grace in the provision of edible
and potable goods *before* the

Figure 5.4. *Expulsion of Adam and Eve from the garden*, 1541,
from Luther's publication of the prophetic books, "Die Proph-
eten alle deudsch."

creation of humanity: God acted creatively and graciously *prior to the
human search for food and drink*. If it were *already* given, there would
be nothing humans could do to merit it. Food and drink are simply

there, there for the use of creatures. Even when the first humans turned away from God and from each other in accusatory blame, the expulsion from Paradise did not herald the loss of food and drink. Rather, the reception of food henceforth would be marked by "sweat," by toil in food production. While humans would no longer enjoy food and drink without work, they would nonetheless continue to receive nourishment through the gift of God and human labor.[50]

Causes of Hunger

While Scripture narrates God's providential offer of food and drink through the medium of creation, the same text also reveals various conditions under which human beings are deprived of daily sustenance. In the ancient Mediterranean world as well as in early modern Saxony, drought and famine were ever-present threats to human life. Where inclement weather or pestilence devastated the growth of the fields and orchards, human beings suffered and frequently perished due to lack of food supplies. Indeed, the Bible chronicles the struggle to survive in the midst of scarcity and the consequent search for food and drink that led people to abandon their homes for other lands. Abraham and Sarah (Gen. 12:10), Isaac (Gen. 16:1-5), Joseph and his family (Gen. 41:53—42:5), Ruth and Naomi (Ruth 1:1-7), David (2 Sam. 21:1), Elijah (1 Kings 18:1-2), and Elisha and the unnamed Shunammite woman (2 Kings 8:1-2) all experienced food shortages that prompted their search for food.

In his commentary on Genesis 26, Luther offered a brief list of disasters that inhibit or stop the growth of produce and the subsequent procurement of food supplies:

> How does it come that such saintly people did not obtain from God the food that was necessary for themselves and for others? For not only Abraham and Isaac but also other very eminent patriarchs and prophets—Jacob, Joseph, Elijah, Elisha, and eventually even Paul and others—had to endure the general disaster of famine together with others. My answer is that God sends famine, wars, pestilence, and similar disasters . . . to try and to test the godly, in order that they may learn to maintain with assurance that they will be

nourished even in a time of famine, even though they are forced to experience various difficulties and, in addition, to look for unknown and uncertain dwelling places.[51]

Here the reformer noted that famine and pestilence may occur as a test of the Christian's faith or as punishment of the wicked;[52] as a test for the faithful (will he or she abandon or assist those in need during a famine?); or as divine judgment upon those who manifest contempt for God and their fellow human beings. Next to famine and pestilence, Luther placed armed conflict as a source of food insecurity. Whether in the ancient world of the Bible or early modern Germany, wars produced the spoliation of crops, loss of farm labor due to military conscription, disruption of economic trade routes, price gouging, artificially inflated interest rates, and the displacement of civilian populations. In the mirror of Scripture, one could see the deleterious effects of war and natural disasters as they eroded or destroyed food supplies and thus rendered a people vulnerable to malnourishment, sickness, and death. "In times of war," he wrote, "we cannot have bread."[53]

Luther claimed that disregard for God and God's commands can produce unnecessary hunger. When King Ahab and Queen Jezebel erected an altar to the Canaanite fertility god, Baal (1 Kings 16:29-34), their faithlessness to the God of Israel brought drought upon the land, a sign of divine punishment. Yet such unbelief or scorn for God also manifested itself socially, in criminal behavior. Coveting a vineyard close to the palace, the two monarchs were able to seize and thus steal Naboth's ancestral vines, his source of income and nourishment (1 Kings 21).[54] Where there is no authentic worship of the one true God, the story suggests, there will be little interest in following the commands of God in relationship to one's neighbor. Indeed, in Luther's various commentaries on the Ten Commandments,[55] he would hold together these two movements: trust in God expressed in the faithful worship of God (encompassing the first three "theological" commandments) directs the good works that benefit the neighbor in need (the seven "social" commandments). Unbelief (*Unglaube*), failing to entrust oneself to God and God's commands as they regulate human interactions, is the root of human injustice (*Ungerechtigkeit*).[56] Where there is no living faith that transforms human self-interest into love for the neighbor and where there is no knowledge of the works of mercy commanded by God, there greed abounds and "evildoers eat up people [just] as they eat bread."[57] In his commentary on the seventh commandment in the "Treatise on Good Works," Luther underscored the role of faith in directing Christian social service: "Faith is the master workman and the motivating force behind the good works of generosity, just as it is in all the other commandments. Without this faith, generosity is of no use at all."[58]

The worship of false gods was not restricted to ancient fertility deities. Luther saw the singular pursuit of wealth as both a theological and a social problem. "It is exceedingly difficult for a rich person to be righteous and godly, because idolatry and contempt for one's brother are associated with wealth."[59] When the pursuit of wealth becomes the false idol worshipped within one's heart, then every other aspect of life, especially one's social relationships, is ordered to that fundamental orientation. While Luther could admit, at times reluctantly, that rich people can use wealth in service to their neighbors, he would also argue that the temptation is strong, almost overwhelmingly so, "to plot against the property of others" and "rob not only by omission but also by commission." One common danger for all people, including the wealthy, "is the sin of omission, when they do not come to the aid of the poor and needy, even though God has sternly commanded (Isa. 58:7): 'Share your bread with the hungry, and bring the homeless poor into your house.' " If those with means fail in this regard, he continued, they will hear the "sad verdict" spoken by Christ: "[To] everyone whom much is given, much will be required" (Luke 12:48).[60] Without the direction of the Holy Spirit, that is, without faith, the rich are simply unbelievers. "The ungodly person robs God of his glory, does not give thanks to God, and refuses aid to the poor. A rich person who is without faith does the same thing. Therefore, he is ungodly."[61] The rich man who "feasted sumptuously every day" was not condemned for his riches but because he sinned by omission: he did not feed the hungry man sitting at his gate. "He was not damned because he robbed or did evil with respect to these goods. . . . He was damned rather because he did not do good to his neighbor, namely, Lazarus. This parable adequately teaches us that it is not sufficient merely not to do evil and not to do harm, but rather that one must be helpful and do good. It is not enough to 'depart from evil.' One must also 'do good' [Ps. 37:27]."[62]

Luther quoted Ambrose of Milan in his commentary on Psalm 118: "Feed the hungry: if you do not feed him, then as far as you are concerned, you have killed him."[63] Here he echoes early Christian, rabbinic, and medieval Christian commentary on the fifth and seventh commandments: one "kills" and "steals" not only by an act of commission (i.e., murdering another human being or stealing what rightfully belongs to another person) but also by an act of omission: failing to provide the hungry with the means to survive. One not only "steals" life from another by actively hoarding food for oneself or one's family but also by passively observing the misery of the hungry poor, by failing to do good when God has clearly commanded it.

Feeding the Hungry as an Act of Hospitality

If the Bible presents a range of factors that cause hunger and imperil life—drought, pestilence, war, theft, greed, laziness, and disobedience—it also teaches the "good work" of feeding the hungry through a variety of exemplars. For instance, Luther praised Abraham and Sarah as a "church" in which the proper use of one's goods was displayed.[64] In his commentary on the story of the three visitors fed by Sarah and Abraham (Gen. 18:1-8), he spoke of the "church" as a "refuge of the exiles and the poor" who roam about "in misery, thirst, hunger," a community that is "constrained to practice works of mercy, to feed the hungry and the thirsty, to receive exiles hospitably, to comfort prisoners, and to visit the sick."[65] On the one hand, Luther will assert that "there is hospitality wherever the church is. For the church, if I may say so, always has a common treasury, inasmuch as it has the command

Figure 5.5. *Abraham and Sarah feed three visitors*, 1670, from a French work on the history of the Bible.

(Matt. 5:42): 'Give to him who begs from you.' "[66] At the same time he will note the possibility of failure: "The church can . . . be indifferent to these difficulties of the brethren."[67]

As a form of hospitality, food and drink are to be provided to Christians who are in peril due to their confession of faith. Likewise, evangelical pastors who no longer receive fees for sacramental or ritual services and languish without state or congregational support are to be fed.[68] Hospitality is to be extended "chiefly to those whom Christ (Matt. 25:40) calls 'the least,' "[69] to the hungry poor of one's city or region. And this, too: food and drink are to be offered to strangers who are in need, even if the stranger be a Turk; one is called to feed friend and enemy alike, the hungry German Christian as well as the hungry Muslim soldier.[70] For Luther Abraham and Sarah thus served as exemplars of both faith in God and service to the stranger in need.

> This is what Abraham does here. He sees these strangers. He does not know who they are; but he does know and see that they are poor and that they are tired from the journey. Therefore he quickly fetches water, washes the feet of the guests, orders a calf to be slaughtered, bread to be prepared, and drink to be fetched. But just as he unknowingly receives the Lord Himself in a hospitable manner, so we, too, when we show some kindness to the least in the kingdom of God, receive Christ Himself in a hospitable manner when He comes to us in the persons of His poor.[71]

While Luther asked individuals, churches, and rulers to discern carefully between the authentically hungry and the panhandler or begging mendicant—"Caution is needed so that we may be aware of vagrants"—the Christian is nonetheless to practice this form of hospitality expansively and without discrimination even though he or she knows that some people will take advantage of such generosity. As Abraham ran to meet his guests who were in need of his household's goods, so Christians are to be generous in the same way, "to open the door to the poor and receive them joyfully." Of course the risk is ever present that cunning and ungrateful people will abuse the Christian's offer of food and drink. "Well and good," writes Luther. "In spite of this our good will is demonstrated to God and the kind act is . . . not lost on Christ, in whose name we are generous."[72]

Management of a National Food Supply

Joseph is praised for the creation of a national food assistance program. Although he was the object of his siblings' envy and "lost his authority in his father's house" (Gen. 37), he nonetheless was elevated to a position of political and social power by the imperial ruler of Egypt after he successfully interpreted Pharaoh's dreams concerning seven years of plenty and seven years of famine (Gen. 41:1-45). Appointed as the supervisor of a food storage and distribution program ("I have set you over the land of Egypt"), Joseph ensured that an abundance of bread was available for sale during famine (Gen. 41:46-57). "It is a great favor to keep so many thousands of people from perishing or to save at least the majority," wrote Luther.[73] Not only did Joseph's food policies save the Egyptian populace from starvation, but they also ensured that other nations would benefit from his wisdom: "All the world came to Joseph in Egypt to buy grain, because the famine

Figure 5.6. *Joseph oversees the storage of grain*, 1573, from a 16th c. edition of the Bible.

became severe throughout the world" (41:57). Luther praised Joseph because he trusted in the God of Israel for guidance. He called him a "teacher of the promises of God" and a wise person who was guided by the Holy Spirit.[74] As a counselor to Pharaoh, Joseph reminded him of the ruler's duty to ensure that the necessities of life be made available to the people. "It becomes the princes to provide for the poor, and especially those who are in their earliest years, lest they perish from hunger. Thus Joseph advised the king."[75] His counsel and his actions obtained a blessing for the world, Luther noted, and saved his envious brothers, his family, and his father, Jacob, who thought him dead.

Labor to Secure Food

Jacob is also praised as an exemplar for Christians. Faced with famine and hearing of the ample grain stores in distant Egypt, he said to his children, "Buy grain for us there, that we may live and not die" (Gen. 42:2). Luther asked the rhetorical question, why does Jacob, the father of Joseph, not trust God to provide food? He even asked with some incredulity, "Where is your faith now, Jacob?" Yet he was quick to answer: "We are ordered to believe and to trust in the goodness of God, but not to tempt God. For we cannot live our life according to the rule which he himself has, but we must live as opportunities and time decide. . . . Although there is no doubt that God is willing to nourish and defend you, you must not avoid the opportunities offered for help."[76] If at all possible, nourishment must be sought through work. Human labor—not wishful thinking or the expectation of miracles—is to provide the necessities of life. "The field must be cultivated, and the produce must be gathered."[77] God promises to nourish and preserve life but wants humans to use the means that are at hand. Roasted chickens, he quips, will not fall out of the sky into the mouths of pious people who are lazy and slothful.[78]

In his Scripture commentaries Luther draws the reader's attention to the many who received physical sustenance from God and provided food and drink for the hungry: Adam and Eve (Gen. 1:29-30; 2:15-18; 3:17-19),[79] Noah and the creatures (Gen. 6:21-22),[80] Abraham and Sarah (Gen 18:1-8),[81] Joseph and the Egyptians (Gen. 41:1-57),[82] Moses and the Hebrews (Deut. 8:1-10),[83] the widow of Zarephath and Elijah (1 Kings 17:8-16),[84] and Elisha (2 Kings 4:42-44).[85] He points to the prophet who condemned the wealthy for "eating up" the poor person's land (Amos 5:10-13)[86] and another who urged the people to share their bread with the hungry, the

Figure 5.7. *God feeds the Hebrews with manna*, 1522, from Luther's pamphlet on the reception of the sacraments with both elements.

fast that is pleasing to God (Isa. 58:6-7).[87] Their protests found voice in Luther's writing: "How much trouble there now is in the world simply on account of those who . . . wantonly oppress the poor and deprive them of their daily bread!"[88] And then this: "Beware! God will not ask you at your death and at the Last Day how much you have left in your will, whether you have given so and so much to churches . . . he will say to you, 'I was hungry, and you gave me no food; I was naked, and you did not clothe me' [Matt. 25:42-43]. Take these words to heart! The important thing is whether you have given to your neighbor and treated him well."[89]

Christ Offers Food and Drink to the Hungry

By invoking the judgment scene narrated in Matthew 25, Luther pointed to Jesus Christ, the gift of God and the exemplar for the Christian in his or her response to the hungry poor. His close reading of the Gospels and his use of the historical or plain sense of Scripture enabled Luther to recognize in the humanity of Christ the experience of human hunger and thirst: "I am talking about [Mary feeding her breast milk to Jesus] so that we may have a foundation for our faith and that we let Christ be a natural human being, in every respect exactly as we are."[90] Throughout his life Christ knew hunger and thirst (Matt. 4:2; 21:18; Mark 11:12; Luke 4:2; John 19:28). In his birth he experienced the pangs of hunger just as in his death he cried out, "I am thirsty."[91] Between these two expressions of Christ's solidarity with humanity in its fundamental physical need, Luther recognized that Christ responded to physical hunger: he ensured that five thousand people received food (Matt. 14:15-21; Mark 6:35-44; Luke 9:12-17; John 6:5-13); he defended his hungry followers when they plucked grain and ate it on the Sabbath (Matt. 12:1-8; Mark 2:23—3:6; Luke 6:1-5); he spoke of outcasts unexpectedly invited to a great banquet (Matt. 22:1-14; Luke 14:16-24); he warned against religious leaders who "devour" the poor (Mark 12:38-40); and he promised that God will fill the hungry (Luke 6:21). Christ offered bread, that is, food and more than food.[92] Thus, in his explanation of the fourth petition of the Lord's Prayer, "Give us this day our daily bread" (Matt. 6:11; Luke 11:3), Luther commented on the gift of food but then expanded its meaning:

Here we consider the poor bread-basket—the needs of our body and our life on earth. It is a brief and simple word, but very comprehensive. When you pray for "daily bread," you pray for everything that is necessary in order to have and enjoy daily bread and, on the contrary, against everything that interferes with enjoying it. You must therefore enlarge and extend your thoughts to include not only the oven or the flour bin, but also the broad fields and the whole land which produce and provide for us our daily bread and all kinds of sustenance. For if God did not cause grain to grow and did not bless and preserve it in the field, we could never take a loaf of bread from the oven to set on the table.

To put it briefly, this petition includes everything that belongs to our entire life in this world; only for its sake do we need daily bread. Now, our life requires not only food and clothing and other necessities for our body, but also peace and concord in our daily business and in associations of every description with the people among whom we live and move— in short, everything that pertains to the regulation of our domestic and our civil or political affairs. For where these two relations are interfered with and prevented from functioning properly, there the necessities of life are also interfered with, and life itself cannot be maintained for any length of time.[93]

Figure 5.8. Workshop of Lucas Cranach, *Apostles' Creed,* 1545, from the title page of the first section on the Creed in Luther's "Small Catechism."

Here Luther considered the social and political context in which the petition is prayed. While Christ promises bread and "all kinds of sustenance" through the agency of creation and human labor, there are forces, nonetheless, that can prevent hungry people from receiving daily sustenance: unjust rulers, war, inflated prices in times of high demand, high interest rates that foster impoverishment, people who refuse to share their abundance. The petition for daily bread not only asks the disciples to pray for bread and to recognize its ultimate source in the Creator but also to pray *against* those conditions and persons that rob people of their daily sustenance: "Defend us from famine and evil men, that they may not deprive us of bread."[94] While elsewhere Luther interpreted "daily bread" in a spiritual sense—as the preaching of the gospel, for instance, or the gift of Christ' sacramental body—his explanations of the fourth petition make clear that one could not avoid real human need and its satisfaction: "What Luther accomplished was something medieval preachers never attempted: the dissolution of the Neoplatonic presupposition that required the material to be placed in subordination to the spiritual. . . . For Luther, the life which daily bread sustained was good in itself, a gift from God given even to the wicked."[95]

Christ's Invitation to Feed the Hungry

With patristic and medieval preachers, Luther focused the attention of his listeners on the works of mercy narrated in one of Jesus' judgment parables:

> When the Son of Man comes in his glory, and all the angels with him, then he will sit on the throne of his glory. All the nations will be gathered before him, and he will separate people one from another as a shepherd separates the sheep from the goats, and he will put the sheep at his right hand and the goats at the left.
>
> Then the king will say to those at his right hand, "Come, you that are blessed by my Father, inherit the kingdom prepared for you from the foundation of the world; for I was hungry and you gave me food, I was thirsty and you gave me something to drink, I was a stranger and you welcomed me, I was naked and you gave me clothing, I was sick and you took care of me, I was in prison and you visited me." Then the righteous will answer him, "Lord, when was it that we saw you hungry and gave you food, or thirsty and gave you something to drink? And when was it that we saw you a stranger and

welcomed you, or naked and gave you clothing? And when was it that we saw you sick or in prison and visited you?" And the king will answer them, "Truly I tell you, just as you did it to one of the least of these who are members of my family, you did it to me."

Then he will say to those at his left hand, "You that are accursed, depart from me into the eternal fire prepared for the devil and his angels; for I was hungry and you gave me no food, I was thirsty and you gave me nothing to drink, I was a stranger and you did not welcome me, naked and you did not give me clothing, sick and in prison and you did not visit me." Then they also will answer, "Lord, when was it that we saw you hungry or thirsty or a stranger or naked or sick or in prison, and did not take care of you?" Then he will answer them, "Truly I tell you, just as you did not do it to one of the least of these, you did not do it to me." And these will go away into eternal punishment, but the righteous into eternal life. (Matt. 25:31-46)

One could not hear a clearer identification of the Son of Man with human suffering or miss the invitation extended to those who give food to the hungry, or fail to notice the chilling condemnation of those who ignored the needs of "the least of these." While he experienced hunger pangs, taught his disciples to pray for daily bread, and gave food to the hungry poor, Jesus also identified himself with anyone—anyone—who is hungry: "Just as you did it to one of the least of these ... you did it to me." In this text Christ not only points to the hungry poor as recipients of charity, but also invites the reader to recognize his hidden presence among those who are

Figure 5.9. *The Day of Judgment*, 1545, from a commentary by Luther on the epistles and gospels appointed for the Sundays from Easter to the beginning of Advent.

hungry, thirsty, strangers, naked, sick, and imprisoned. "We, too, when we show some kindness to the least in the kingdom of God, receive Christ himself in a hospitable manner when he comes to us in the person of his poor."[96]

Yet discernment is required of the Christian. The members of religious orders who boast of outward poverty should not receive alms or food because such charity only supports a religious conviction that is false: "sacred poverty" and "holy hunger" (that is, fasting) merit nothing in the eyes of God. The very notion that hunger and poverty hold some kind of "spiritual" value is to be banished. Luther argued that poverty and hunger are debilitating conditions that merit remedies rather than the patina of "holiness." Poverty is not to be "recommended, chosen, or taught; for there is always enough of that by itself." Rather, "Christ commands that . . . poverty be cared for and improved among our neighbors."[97] True religion, faith active in works of loving service, should be practiced by Christians so that Christ no longer would need to cry out in the voices of those who are hungry, thirsty, without shelter, naked, and sick.[98] At the same time Christians should not be led to believe that endowments or gifts to religious institutions such as schools, monasteries, or churches will gain them any favor in the sight of God. Furthermore, their gift is empty if it is offered to secure a reputation among men and women. "Christ, at the last day, will not ask how much you have done this or that for yourself, but how much good you have done to others, even to the very least (Matt. 25:40, 45)."[99] God does not need charity, endowments, or gifts; rather, the neighbor does, that "we may be of benefit only to others and to their salvation."[100] Christians who seek to further their public prestige under the pretense of charitable gifts to hospitals or food distribution centers "will hear a stern judgment on the Last Day, when Christ will accuse them of persecuting him."[101]

Employing the central axiom of the reform, Luther linked the teaching on justification by grace, passive and social righteousness, Christ as gift and example with Christian public service in a forceful argument that asked after the *motive* that prompts Christian concern for the hungry poor. To highlight faith in God's unconditional grace as the active guide and "supervisor" of Christian good works, Luther questioned a social ethic rooted simply and solely in rewards and punishments and entertained the possibility that the Christian, under the influence of grace, would actually serve the neighbor in need because such service benefited the neighbor. He wrote that on the Last Day, "[Christ] will praise the deeds of kindness we have done for the poor (Matt. 25:31-46)."[102] It is interesting that he did not say that Christ will "reward" human kindness or "punish" the greedy or duplicitous. Perhaps he held out the possibility that even on the Last Day one can consciously persist in sin against other human beings and thus receive the "reward" for such sin: an eternity of self-absorption, cut off from God and others. On the other hand, faith is to be made manifest in works of love directed toward the welfare and well-being of one's neighbor.

Christ's Invitation to Parents and Political Leaders

We do not need to search far to find persons in need of food and shelter: they reside in our homes. The first duty of every parent is to ensure that his or her child receives food and drink, clothing, shelter, and proper medical care. The home itself is a "hospital," a place in which we practice "hospitality" toward the most vulnerable: needy children dependent on their parents for both physical and spiritual nourishment.

> If parents rightly train [their children] to God's service, they will indeed have their hands full of good works. For what are the hungry, the thirsty, the naked, the sick, the alien if not . . . your own children? With these God makes a hospital of your own house. He sets you over them as the hospital superintendent, to wait on them, to give them the food and drink of good words and works. . . . How many good works you have at hand in your own home with your own children who need all such things as these like a hungry, thirsty, naked, poor, imprisoned, sick soul. . . . What use is it if [parents] fast themselves to death, pray, or go on pilgrimages? God will not ask them about these . . . on the day of judgment, but will require of them the children entrusted to their care.[103]

The feeding of one's child or children is not to be exercised when it suits the needs or schedule of mother and father. The parental office is not a matter of pleasure or whim but a "strict commandment and injunction of God" that will hold parents accountable for the welfare of their children on the Last Day.[104] While Luther presented the honor and obedience children are to offer their parents in this, his explanation of the Fourth Commandment, he was also quick to point out the social dynamic: parents hold power over their children. This "right to govern," however, is not to be exercised in such a way that the parent elicits the homage or brute obedience of the child.[105] Rather, this "office" or

power must be exercised in service to the welfare of the child or children, a service that is to be guided by the invitation of Christ to care for the most vulnerable in one's home.

What obtains in the home is to be mirrored in the state: the ruler is to care for all people by ensuring that the "necessities of life," especially the food supply, are secured and maintained. While Luther found justification for his claim in the story of the pharaoh who ordered Joseph to supervise the Egyptian food stores, he also praised his own prince, Frederick of Saxony, who "not only provided for public barns and granaries" and the preparation of field storage trenches but also ensured that grain and wine were stored in ample amount in the event of drought or pestilence.[106] Where there is manifest need, the ruler or political leader is to be ever watchful so that no one goes hungry and that ample stores are maintained to prevent food shortages. "It becomes the princes to provide for the poor, and especially those who are in their earliest years, lest they perish from hunger."[107] If the home can be imagined

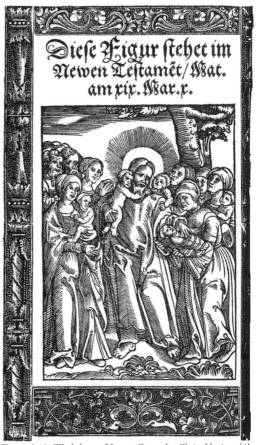

Figure 5.10. Workshop of Lucas Cranach, *Christ blessing children*, 1545, from Luther's "Small Catechism."

as a "hospital" that cares for children, so too can the princely region be likened to a hospital—a place of civic hospitality—in which the prince as a political "patron" supervises the governmental projects that respond to the basic necessities of life. "It would therefore be fitting if the coat-of-arms of every upright prince were emblazoned with a loaf of bread instead of a lion or a wreath, or if a loaf of bread were stamped on coins, to remind both princes and subjects that through the office of the princes we enjoy protection and peace and that without them we could not have the steady blessing of daily bread."[108]

Just as parents are to feed their children and provide them with clothing, housing, medical needs, and an elementary education, so the prince is to ensure that peace is kept so that fields and orchards may produce food, that food storage centers are maintained for the people, and that food is distributed to persons with genuine need (the poor, widows, the sick) and to anyone suffering during a time of war, drought, or pestilence. Ensuring that food is available for people in need, "especially those in their earliest years," is the responsibility of the individual Christian, of parents in their home, of Christian communities, and of the ruler, not one or the other. It is a political duty, for Luther, inspired by the example of virtuous rulers in the Bible and Christ's invitation to all Christians, including Christian leaders, to feed the hungry and give drink to the thirsty, to welcome the stranger and care for the sick. To imagine the home or political society as a "hospital" is to focus parent and ruler on the support of life. "There is no greater praise of hospitality than that in Matt. 25:35: 'I was hungry, and you gave Me bread.' "[109]

In the context of sixteenth-century Germany, the vast majority of the population was Christian as were all the regional rulers. Luther spoke of princely duties in terms of biblical exemplars—Joseph, David, and Solomon, for instance—knowing that his vernacular translations of the Bible were promoted and even read by his own rulers. In his appeal for the reform of church and society as inspired by his reading of the Bible in light of the signs of his own time, he could encourage the princes of Germany to fulfill their Christian duties. Likewise, he could preach and write about the duty of Christians and Christian parents to feed their children and their needy neighbors because this "work of mercy" was taught and commanded by Scripture, that is, by various figures in the history of Israel and by Jesus, the Word of God. Yet that image of Christ as the living "speaking" of God to humanity, so prominent in his theological project, was not the only metaphor through which Luther interpreted Jesus Christ. He also knew him as the one who continued to give himself as living food and drink in the form of bread broken and eaten and wine shared and sipped, in that fragment of an ancient Jewish meal the young Luther knew as the Mass and the reformer would eventually call the Lord's Supper.

6
HOLDING ALL THINGS IN COMMON

The Eucharist and Social Welfare

A careful reading of the Bible reveals that Jews and Christians have known something about bread, food and drink, and meals celebrated in the presence of God. In the Sabbath supper, Passover, the meals of Jesus, and the table practice of the first Christians, theological and social relationships can be discerned. These meals suggest who needs food and who gives food, why and when meals are to be kept, and how food is to be shared. As a student of the Bible, Martin Luther was familiar with the many meals of the Bible and could discern the meanings of meals as symbolic and historical realities. Yet Luther was not only a student and a teacher of the Bible, he also served as a priest and then a pastor who presided at the Christian community's celebration of the Mass, the Lord's Supper. While fragments of his biblical commentaries reveal, in outline, a social ethic focused on the hungry poor, his practice and reform of the Mass also emerged as a significant matrix in which a Christian response to food insecurity was set forth. "Between the sacraments on the one hand and an ethical life on the other, Luther saw a profound connection."[1]

Sharing Common Property

If, in 1517, one could read in Luther's Ninety-five Theses his early concern for the hungry poor, his thought continued to develop as he commented on and suggested food practices rooted in that meal that had attracted so many names: the breaking of the bread, Lord's Supper,

Mass, sacrament of the altar, divine service. Among his earliest works on the Mass was a statement addressed in 1519 to a laywoman, Margaret, Duchess of Brunswick. In this treatise Luther compared the ecclesial practice of the Mass with the social practice of German religious lay fraternities called "brotherhoods." Within six months of the statement's publication, Pope Leo X included the work in a catalog of Luther's condemned writings, an act that only increased Luther's notoriety in Germany and sharpened the growing division between the nascent reform movement and Roman leadership of the church. The treatise was structured in a tripartite manner focused on three dimensions of the sacrament: the outward *sign*, the *significance* or effect of the sacrament, and the *role of faith* in the sacrament. Through the lens of his sacramental commentary, Luther concluded the treatise with a critique of the practices of the religious brotherhoods and an early proposal for sharing food with the hungry poor.

In 1519 the city of Wittenberg counted twenty lay religious fraternities, a sizable number for the city but small in comparison to the 127 listed in Hamburg. Tracing their origin to the German *Schützgilden*, the religious brotherhoods of the late Middle Ages were founded to meet the spiritual and social needs of their members during life and at death. Dues were regularly paid to the fraternity, money that was intended to support brotherhood activities and fraternal assistance: monthly dinners and masses, members who were unemployed or in need of funds due to illness, and a range of services at death. Such lay brotherhoods functioned not only as social clubs but also as burial societies: fees collected would pay for a proper burial mass and the recitation of a number of prepaid masses to ensure that the deceased was released more rapidly from the purgative state into union with God. Of course, those who possessed greater wealth would benefit more rapidly from the "investment" in this financial "service" than those of more modest means.

It is in this context that Luther applied his understanding of the sacrament of Christ's "holy and true body" to the religious and social practices of the brotherhoods. Following earlier Christian understanding, Luther wrote that a sacrament consists in an external or material sign—bread and wine in the Mass and water in baptism—signs, furthermore, that need to be used: food and drink are given to be consumed by the recipient. The sacrament must be received, not merely looked at, "if it is to work a blessing."[2] The effect or significance of the sacrament received by the individual and the community, he claimed, is "the fellowship of all that saints."[3] Those who receive the bread and wine are bound socially and spiritually to each other and to Christ who gives nourishment to his body, the Christian community. Drawing on an urban metaphor, Luther compared the spiritual body or communion to the inhabitants of a city, "each citizen being a member of the other and of the entire city,"[4] When one receives bread and wine, one receives a "sure sign of fellowship" with Christ and all the saints. One is drawn into or confirmed in one's citizenship in a public, social, and spiritual communion ("spiritual" since its animating presence is the Spirit of the risen Christ), a community in which gifts and services are shared among the members.[5]

In the Mass bread is broken from one loaf and given to each person; wine is sipped from one cup. The reception of this shared bread and cup not only signify membership, one's public identity as a Christian, but also a sharing of spiritual possessions, of spiritual "goods," between Christ and the community and among members of the community. These "possessions" Luther referred to as "common property."[6] Again, Luther used the image of a city

Figure 6.1. Workshop of Lucas Cranach, *The sacrament of Holy Communion*, 1545, from the section on the Sacrament of Communion in Luther's "Small Catechism."

to elucidate the meaning of sharing possessions. "It is like a city where every citizen shares with all the others the city's name, honor, freedom,

trade, customs, usages, help . . . while at the same time he shares all the
dangers of fire and flood, enemies and death, losses, taxes, and the like.
For he who would share in the profits must also share in the costs, and
ever recompense love with love."[7] If one citizen is injured, all citizens
suffer injury to their collective "body." If one citizen benefits all the
other citizens, then thanks are offered to the benefactor by all. It is so in
the Christian community, Luther wrote: if one member suffers, Christ
and all the baptized suffer; if one member is honored, Christ and all
the baptized rejoice. If one is assailed with spiritual or physical suffering, "go to the sacrament of the altar," he advised, "and lay down [your]
woe in the midst of the community and seek help from the entire
company . . . just as a citizen whose property has suffered damages
makes complaint to the town council."[8] Just as Christ shared in the
misery and joy of humanity and offered his life to and for humanity as
the "sure sign" and "token" of God's salvific purposes, so the Christian
community, nourished with the "gifts" of Christ, bears the responsibility to share its "goods" with all others.

> When you have partaken of this sacrament, therefore, or desire
> to partake of it, you must in turn share the misfortunes of the
> fellowship. . . . Here your heart must go out in love and learn that
> this is a sacrament of love. As love and support are given you, you in
> turn must render love and support to Christ in his needy ones. You
> must feel with sorrow all the dishonor done to Christ in his holy
> Word, all the misery of Christendom, all the unjust suffering of the
> innocent, with which the world is everywhere filled to overflowing.
> You must fight, work, pray and . . . have heartfelt sympathy. . . .
> Here the saying of Paul is fulfilled, "Bear one another's burdens, and
> so fulfill the law of Christ" [Gal. 6:2].[9]

Luther suggested that receiving bread and wine, the body and blood
of Christ, signifies the creation or confirmation of a community that
receives "gifts" and consequently bears responsibility to respond in
mutual assistance to each other. One not only receives but shares that
which has been given freely. Such mutual sharing is not an option; it is a
sure sign of a lively and living faith. Here one can discern an allusion to
his distinction between "alien righteousness" received from without and

"proper righteousness" expressed in service to one's neighbor. "Offer to others your strength, as if it were their own, just as Christ does for you in the sacrament. This is what it means to be changed into one another through love, out of many particles to become one bread and drink."[10]

This mutual sharing in the benefits and dangers that accompany citizenship in the Christian fellowship can be understood as a source of strength and consolation. Luther was clear in noting the manifold sufferings that assail humanity, the Christian, and the church. There is no guarantee, he claimed, that faith, "on which everything depends," will stand firm in the midst of such suffering. As the capacity to trust another's promise, faith enables the baptized who suffer doubt, temptation, or anxiety to grasp the promise that Christ and all the saints are with them. "Do not doubt that you have what the sacrament signifies, that is, be certain Christ and all his saints are coming to you with all their virtues, sufferings, and mercies, to live, work, suffer and die with you, and that they desire to be wholly yours, having all things in common with you."[11] Faith is the capacity to recognize, to *see* these realities and to trust them. At the same time one's faith is nourished by participation in this common meal, for one receives not only bread and wine but the renewing presence of the living Christ who offers his strength in exchange for human frailty, his magnanimous love in exchange for human selfishness. "By means of this sacrament, all self-seeking love is rooted out and gives place to that which seeks the common good of all; and through the change wrought by love there is one bread, one drink, one body, one community."[12]

For Luther there could be no sacrament without an external or material sign instituted by Christ. Thus, bread and wine—food and drink—are to be received and consumed. Such eating and drinking are intended to effect something in the recipients—their being repeatedly drawn into the community or fellowship of Christ and all the baptized, a community marked by a free sharing of "gifts" or "possessions." And such eating and drinking is to be done in faith—faith in its Pauline sense as "trust" and in its Johannine sense as "sight"—a seeing that recognizes in the material sign the presence of Christ, a trusting that clings to the promise of Christ's presence with the community.

It is from this particular sacramental perspective that Luther analyzed the religious fraternities found in the urban centers of Germany and western Europe. He recognized that such fraternities or guilds could be sources of genuine assistance to their members: they could promote a particular craft, train younger people in a viable livelihood, offer assistance to the widows and children of deceased members, lead efforts at collective bargaining, and assist the sick or unemployed. Were it only so, he lamented. While he noted that a brotherhood may portray itself publicly as a "special convocation of good works," they had become collectors of money for drunken rampages, the city records of Wittenberg confirming Luther's criticism in the enormous fines charged against the carousing brotherhood members for their destruction of public and private property. His sharpest criticism, however, was aimed at the inner-focused character of these associations: they tended to care only for themselves and ignore those who were hungry or poor in the larger urban landscape. They did this with a patina of religious approval since they paid for masses and sponsored "spiritual" practices. "In the [brotherhoods]," he wrote, "[people] learn to seek

Figure 6.2. The parable of the great banquet, 1563, from a later edition of one of Luther's church postills.

their own good, to love themselves, to be faithful only to one another, to stand higher before God than others."[13] While the brotherhoods may have offered food, shelter, and medical care to the members and their families, they actually gave their members the impression that the act of giving itself was more important than the person in need. "It was not the poor person who counted," wrote Louis Chatellier in his study of early modern charity, "but the *act* accomplished in the sight of God or for the good of the [institution of the] church."[14] Why be concerned with the hungry person if the primary focus was an act of charitable giving that would accrue benefits, spiritual or social, to the benefactor? The hand *offering* food or alms to the hungry would be of far greater importance than the hand *receiving* food.

"In the [brotherhoods] men learn to seek their own good, to love themselves, to be faithful only to one another, to despise others, to think themselves better than others and to presume to stand higher before God than others. And so perishes the communion of saints, Christian love, and the true brotherhood which is established in the holy sacrament."[15] The complaint heard in Luther's sermon "Two Kinds of Righteousness" and the instruction "What to Look for and Expect in the Gospels"—confusing God's action and human work—entered this early treatise on the Mass. The sacrament should not be viewed as the means through which one approaches, comes closer to, or seeks favor with God. "This is the fault of the preachers who do not preach the gospel or the sacrament, but their humanly devised fables about the many works [of satisfaction] to be done."[16] Rather, the Mass is the means through which Christ comes to the Christian community and offers his possessions, his "goods," his body as bread, his blood as wine, freely and to anyone who seeks their nourishment. And this, too: food and drink are offered and shared within the Christian community as a model for the sharing of food and drink with the hungry poor of the city. Sacramental practice becomes here a model for imaging social welfare practice.

Luther invoked the liturgical practice of the early Christians "when the sacrament was properly used and the people were taught to understand this fellowship." From the practice of sharing one bread and one cup, "they gathered food and material goods in the church, and there—as St. Paul writes in I Corinthians—distributed among those who were in need. We have a vestige of this [practice] in the little word 'collect' in the mass, which means a general collection, just as a common fund is gathered to be given to the poor."[17] Elsewhere Luther would write that there is no greater service to God than Christian love that helps and serves the needy. "This is why the possessions of the church were formerly called *bona ecclesiae*, that is, common property, a common chest, as it were, for all who were needy among the Christians."[18] The goods of the church are not to be augmented, stored up, or "invested" but given away. Consequently, if the brotherhoods wanted to practice true religion, "they should gather up food and serve a tableful or two of poor people, for the sake of God."[19] In this recommendation Luther was calling for those who had adequate means to share a meal with those in need, that is, to share a meal with other human beings who can be known as distinctive persons with real needs rather than anonymous recipients of one's charitable donation. The emphasis seems to shift from perceiving food as a "commodity to be consumed" to food as an "unexpected gift to be received," from "giving for one's own sake" to "recognizing the needs of another person."[20]

This is not to suggest that monasteries and cathedrals—the primary centers of late medieval social welfare and food distribution— were oblivious to the plight of the hungry poor in their surrounding neighborhoods. It is to claim, nonetheless, that Luther diagnosed a pressing motive alive in the late medieval imagination and found it terribly wrong. In the "spiritual economy" of the late Middle Ages, good works, charitable giving, the administration of social welfare, and the Mass itself could all be understood as *means to achieve another end*— that is, the securing of one's eternal destiny in a heavenly world or the public enhancement of one's reputation in this world. Both concerns focused on the actions of the elite benefactor rather than the hungry poor person and his or her needs.

Here we can recognize the significance of the teaching on justification by grace as Luther used it in his interpretation of the Bible, the sacraments, and social welfare: the first salvific "movement," the first impulse to bestow "life, health, and salvation" originates in God, the movement or advance of God toward a world of great need and immeasurable suffering. Such a movement becomes "flesh" in the incarnation of the Word of God who embodies and discloses the intentions of God toward the creation. As Luther would write elsewhere,[21] the Mass—the Lord's Supper—is nothing less than Christ's last will and "new testament" to his followers in every generation. In the sacramental actions God continues to move toward humanity in the speaking, washing, and eating directed ("instituted") by Christ to awaken the baptized continually to "faith in God" and to "love for the neighbor in need." In his statement on the brotherhoods, Luther offers a first and admittedly simple proposal that underscores this theological reorientation: the Christian community continues this movement toward humanity's need by making a general collection, a common fund, of food and material goods to be shared with the hungry poor.

Responding to the hungry neighbor was no longer to be the responsibility of religious orders or priests in a cathedral. Given Luther's insistence, articulated in the "Address to the Christian Nobility of the German Nation," that there is one "spiritual estate" comprising all the baptized, the members of the local congregation or parish are charged with responding to the evidence of food insecurity. It is the responsibility of all baptized Christians to know their neighbors and their neighbors' needs. At the same time the brotherhoods, composed of baptized Christians, can gather provisions

Figure 6.3. *Christ waiting for the people after the supper,* 1588, from a later edition of Luther's "Hausspostilla."

and serve meals at tables of poor people "for the sake of God." A "true fast" or "true religion," as he noted elsewhere,[22] is expressed in sharing one's bread with the hungry. This is what it means to do something "for the sake of God"—one's actions benefit another human being. Clearly, God does not need the gospel or bread; humans beings, however, need both. Rather than serve only the needs of their own "kind," the brotherhoods are to expand their concern to anyone who is hungry and poor.

In effect Luther marshaled biblical evidence (e.g., Paul's description of early Christian meal practice; collections for the hungry in time of famine), his theological convictions (e.g., "alien" and "proper" righteousness; Christ as *donum* and *exemplum*), and his emerging reflection on the Christian meal practice (i.e., the Mass) to propose not only liturgical and sacramental reform but also a reorientation in social ethics. That is, Luther not only recognized but insisted on a profound relationship between the liturgical celebration of the sacraments and the promotion of a social ethic in daily life with its many pressing needs and issues. This suggests that public policy (e.g., responding to the hungry poor) was shaped by biblical, sacramental, and theological convictions. Bible, liturgy, theology, and ethics—while distinguished—could not be separated from each other into discrete compartments. In both worship and ethics, for instance, the central teaching on justification by grace served as the pivotal principle in the reform.[23] "Luther's social ethics in general and his social welfare activity in particular may be understood as a work of the people flowing from worship."[24] Indeed, Luther could readily see that one of the primary functions of the sacramental celebration was to challenge a self-seeking absorption and orient both the Christian and the Christian community outward toward service to the common good in society.

An Offering Not to God but to the Hungry

In the year following the publication of his work on the brotherhoods, Luther set forth his agenda for the reform of the sacraments in "The Babylonian Captivity of the Church," a work that would signal his fundamental break with the medieval interpretation and practice of the sacraments. The title of this extended work was inspired by the biblical account of the conquest of Judah in the sixth century BCE: as the Jews were captured and taken from Jerusalem into exile under the Babylonian ruler, so Christians—he claimed—had been carried away from their native land, Scripture, by the tyrannical power of the Roman papacy. Without the study of Scripture, argued Luther, the sacraments have been subjected to a faulty theology and misused by the few at the expense of the many. The sacraments "have been subjected to a miserable captivity by the Roman curia, and the church has been robbed of all her liberty."[25] Luther examined each of the seven "papal" sacraments—"the bread," baptism, penance, confirmation, marriage, ordination, and extreme unction—and argued that only baptism, Eucharist, and penance were instituted by Christ and could be celebrated as sacraments. The other four might be significant Christian rituals and should be retained as such, but without a clear institution by Christ, an external sign, and a promise attached to them, they could not be considered sacraments. In this comprehensive treatment of the sacramental system, his lengthiest commentary concerns "the bread," the Lord's Supper, of which he speaks first.

Attacking the medieval practice of withholding the cup of wine from the laity, Luther argued that Scripture clearly notes that both bread and wine should be given to every Christian. "The word and example of Christ stand unshaken when he says, not by way of permission, but of command: 'Drink of it, all of you' [Matt. 26:27]. . . . If the words cannot be understood as addressed to the priest alone, then it certainly is an impious act to withhold the cup from the laymen."[26] From this first "captivity" of the sacrament, Luther proceeded to the second: the medieval use of Aristotelian categories to understand or explain how the bread and wine of the Mass "become" the body and blood of Christ. The incorporation of the philosophical distinction between accident (i.e., bread) and substance (i.e., body) produced "that Babel of a philosophy of a constant quantity distinct from the substance, until it has come to such a pass that they themselves no longer know what are accidents and what is substance."[27] For Luther Greek philosophy had come to overshadow the study and use of Scripture in sacramental theology. Rather than search for "reasonable" explanations that demonstrate how bread is body, Luther argued that one cannot rationally fathom this mystery and must "take reason captive to the obedience of Christ," trust his word, and "firmly believe not only that the body of Christ is in the bread, but that the bread is the body of Christ."[28]

It was what Luther called the "third captivity of this sacrament" that so enraged the reformer. It was "by far the most wicked abuse of all, in consequence of which there is no opinion more generally held . . . than this, that the mass is a good work and a sacrifice. And this

abuse has brought an endless host of other abuses in its train."[29] The
holy sacrament, he complained, had been turned into "mere merchandise, a market, and a profit-making business. Hence participations,
brotherhoods, intercessions, merits, anniversaries, memorial days and
the like wares are bought and sold, traded and bartered, in the church.
On these the priests and monks depend for their livelihood."[30] Luther
directed the reader first to the words of Christ, "in which he instituted
this sacrament," a harmony of several biblical texts included in the
"Captivity" treatise.[31] What is their meaning?

"Let this stand as our first and infallible proposition—the mass
. . . is Christ's testament, which he left behind him at his death to be
distributed among his believers,"[32] that is, the Mass itself is the "new
testament" Christ gives to his own. Drawing on custom and the legal
practice of his time, Luther noted that a testament is a promise, made
by a testator in expectation of his or her death, in which the bequest
and the heirs are designated. In the "Captivity," he claimed that the
"mass is a promise of the forgiveness of sins made to us by God . . .
[and] confirmed with the death of the Son of God."[33] Again, Luther
underscored the divine initiative: the Mass is not a prayer, not a sacrifice, not a work offered to God but the means through which *Christ
offers a testament to humanity, a testament given before it could be sought.*
As a testament freely given, no payment, no work, no merit, no price
could be attached to the Mass. Indeed, Luther condensed the meaning
of the entire Mass into these words: "Take and eat" (Matt. 26:26): food
and drink are given freely for nourishment.[34] When faith trusts and
clings to these words of the Word of God, then follows love, and "love
does every good work, for it does no wrong, indeed, it is the fulfilling of
the law."[35] From *promise*, articulated in the word of Christ and the sign
of bread to trusting *faith* that this word and sign are given "for you," to
love as good works exercised in the world, Luther drew again the divine
initiative that begins in God, is revealed in Christ, is received by the
baptized faithful, and continues into the world of daily life. While he
would admit that prayers are made and people sing to God during the
liturgy, these must be carefully distinguished from the first and essential movement of the Mass: through word and sign, Christ is coming to
the gathered assembly as the sacrament of God's mercy so that, among
other benefits, they might enter the world of human need.

Figure 6.4. *Christ comes to a hungry beggar*, 1523, from a sermon on death by Luther.

Consequently, the liturgical texts of the Mass were to be excised of any language that suggested "sacrifice," "work," or "offering." While Luther would retain the ancient shape of the Mass and its fundamental elements, it was to be reformed in light of the central principle of justification by grace and thus guarded from any language or ritual practice that would suggest that God is the recipient of human endeavor rather than "the dispenser of his own works." In light of this central teaching—the sharp-edged clipper that would prune away the growth of sacrificial language and meaning—the priest who presided was to be understood as a servant who communicates the promise and the sign which are to be received passively in the Mass. Where the Mass is understood as a good work performed to benefit the worker, then it will necessarily but wrongly be construed as the central "transaction" in a spiritual economy that too easily benefits the few and discriminates against the many. And so, concerning the reform of the Mass and the various consequences of this reform, Luther asked himself a question: "Will you not overturn the practice and teaching of all the churches and monasteries, by virtue of which they have flourished all these centuries? For the mass is the foundation of their anniversaries, intercessions, applications, communications, that is to say, of their fat incomes." What alarmed him in 1517, the church-sanctioned sale of spiritual goods and services, appeared in 1520 to be a monstrous deformation of Christ's intention and early Christian practice as recorded in the New Testament:[36] always a sacrament given freely, never a sacrifice enmeshed with the hint or need of payment.

Indeed, Luther would reinterpret the nettlesome term "sacrifice" in a manner similar to his interpretation of "priesthood" in the "Address to the Christian Nobility of the German Nation."

> We are instructed by the Apostle in I Cor. 11[:21, 33] that it was customary for Christ's believers, when they came together for mass, to bring with them food and drink. These they called "collections," and they distributed them among all who were in want, after the example of the apostles in Acts 4[:34–35]. From this store was taken the portion of the bread and wine that was consecrated in the sacrament. And since all this store was consecrated by the word and prayer [I Tim. 4:5], by being "lifted up" according to the Hebrew rite of which we read in Moses [Num. 18:30–32], the words and rite of this lifting up or offering have come down to us. . . . Thus, in Isa. 37[:4] Hezekiah commanded Isaiah to lift up his prayer in the sight of God for the remnant. In the Psalms we read: "Lift up your hands to the holy place" [Ps. 134:2]. And again: "To thee I will lift up my hands" [Ps. 63:4]. And in I Tim. 2[:8]: "In every place lifting holy hands." For this reason the words "sacrifice" and "offering" must be taken to refer not to the sacrament and testament, but to the collections themselves. From this source also the word "collect" has come down to us for the prayers said in the mass.[37]

While "sacrifice" once may have denoted the grain or animal offerings associated with temple worship, the term itself was reinterpreted in light of the gospel of Jesus Christ. Since the sacrifices of the temple ended with Christ's death, so Christians claimed, "sacrifice" was retained but broken of its earlier meaning and, in the metaphorical twist of the New Testament, emerged in a surprisingly new light: "I appeal to you therefore, brothers and sisters, by the mercies of God, to present your bodies as a living sacrifice, holy and acceptable to God, which is your spiritual worship" (Rom. 12:1). Here the apostle Paul exhorted the Christians in Rome to "holy" living exercised in the world; this is the "sacrifice" that God finds pleasing. In his commentary on Romans, Luther wrote that the Christian "sacrifice" is the new and holy life lived by the baptized.[38] Indeed, his summary of Romans 12 simply reads: "The apostle instructs the Romans both in the things which pertain to God as well as those things which pertain to our neighbor." Such holy living flows toward the neighbor. Indeed, "sacrifice," as Luther notes, refers not to the Mass—"the sacrament and testament"—but to the prayers and the collections of food "distributed among all who were in want." A portion of the bread and wine collected at the beginning of Christian gatherings was set aside for the Lord's Supper while the rest was offered at the end to the hungry poor. In effect the people witnessed the relationship between sacrament and society: the gifts of bread and wine given to them as Christ's body and blood and the larger store of bread and wine given to the needy.

Food for the Poor, Sunday and Every Day

Within three years of the publication of "The Babylonian Captivity of the Church," the cities of Augsburg, Nürnberg, Altenburg, Kitzingen, Strassburg, Breslau, and Regensburg were attempting to care for their hungry poor within the context of the "Lutheran" reform. Indeed, the city of Wittenberg had passed legislation concerning worship and social welfare in 1522, one of the earliest of evangelical "church orders" (*Kirchenordnung*).[39] The Wittenberg Order approved the reformed Mass for worship in the city's churches, "as Christ instituted it at the Last Supper." At the same time the order claimed the city's responsibility for those who through age, sickness, or misfortune had fallen into poverty. Included in this group were poor artisans, orphans, the children of poor people, young women in need of a dowry, priests "whom we now have" with no financial support from the recitation of masses, and young students in school. The order also prohibited beggars who would not work or refused training in a trade, begging monks and mendicants (e.g., Dominicans and Franciscans), and foreign university students who could not provide their own food and drink. All the income from churches, brotherhoods, guilds, endowments to priests, and the inventory of precious liturgical items no longer used in the reformed Mass was to be collected into a common chest and then distributed among the hungry poor of the city by two members of the city council, two representatives from the city, and a secretary.

Within a year Luther was asked for his advice on the reform of worship and welfare by leaders in eleven villages that constituted the parish of Leisnig, southeast of Wittenberg. Having received the "Lutheran" reform, the Leisnig parish had called its own pastor, desired to celebrate the evangelical Mass, claimed responsibility for the establishment and funding of schools, and faced the work of caring for its hungry poor. Luther affirmed the "evangelical" town council in its effort to promote a congregational polity, a reformed liturgy, education for all citizens, and an organized initiative for the poor and needy—all four flowing from Luther's teaching on justification by grace and the "priesthood of all the baptized." In 1523 he published in one pamphlet his preface to the town's ordinance or agreement and the text of the ordinance regarding a common chest.[40] At the outset of the preface, the evangelical Christians at Leisnig are praised for acceptance of the reformed Mass and the establishment of "a common fund after the example of the apostles." Set next to and flowing from "the breaking of the bread and the prayers" (Acts 2:42), Luther invoked the social practice of the early Christians: "All who believed were together and had all things in common; they would sell their possessions and goods and distribute the proceeds to all, as any had need" (Acts 2:44-45). Next to the sharing of bread was set the sharing of all things commonly held. The Leisnig common chest—the collection and sharing of goods by the community for distribution "to all, as any had need"—was to be supplemented, in part, by the appropriation of monastic, mendicant, and ecclesial properties. The sale of said properties, the use of their incomes, or their transformation into schools for children or housing for the needy was to be accomplished without force or harm.

Figure 6.5. The Wittenberg Common Chest. Photo © Foto Kirsch, Wittenberg.

> Devote all the remaining property to the common fund of a common chest, out of which gifts and loans could be made in Christian love to all the needy in the land, be they noble or commoners. . . . Now there is no greater service of God than Christian love which helps and serves the needy, as Christ himself will judge and testify at the

Last Day, Matthew 25[:31-46]. This is why the possessions of the church were formerly called *bona ecclesiae*, that is, common property, a common chest, as it were, for all who were needy among the Christians.[41]

At the conclusion of the preface, Luther hoped that his suggestions would diminish begging and the usurious practices that subject the poor and the needy to a lifetime of impoverishment. He also noted the salutary effect of offering one's goods for the common good: giving freely and generously to others can quench a person's greed. If only one or two follow his advice, he would be content. Yet he remained somewhat dubious: "The world must remain the world. . . . I have done what I can. . . . God help us all to do what is right and to stand firm."[42]

The Leisnig Agreement followed Luther's preface and, in its preliminary statement, claimed the congregation's capacity to appoint its own pastor "for the sole purpose of preaching God's word and administering the sacraments," to exercise its Christian liberty in conformity with the Scripture, and to undertake the care of the hungry poor. The right to call a pastor and care for their own needy, the agreement noted, are rooted in "the eternal blessings won by our Lord and Savior Christ out of pure grace and mercy," and "our universal priesthood," implicit echoes of Luther's teaching on justification by grace and his redefinition of the spiritual estate. Since the agreement set forth the community's commitment to social welfare, it declared at the outset that "all the internal and external possessions of Christian believers are to serve and contribute to the honor of God and the love of the fellow-Christian neighbor."[43] Where there is "eternal blessing," there is "brotherly love," and where there is such love, it comes to expression in deeds of kindness directed toward the needy. The love of Christ inspires Christian love of neighbor; the "Christian and evangelical Scriptures" guide social welfare.

The agreement then listed the ecclesial sources of income that, henceforth, would be donated to the common chest: hereditary lands, supplementary rents, toll income from church-owned bridges, cash, silver, jewels, rents from chapels, benefices, revenues, stores, income from masses for the dead, perpetual memorials, income from indulgence sales, alms, income and annuities from brotherhoods, and contributions, penances, or fines paid by craft guilds and peasant farmers to the church.[44] In the space of a few paragraphs, the agreement named the myriad sources of income collected by the late medieval parish, monastery, convent, or priory. Some of this income was distributed to the hungry poor and the needy or used to support hospices and orphanages since cathedral personnel, parish priests, and monastic communities were centers of social welfare in the late medieval world. At the same time the list reveals the many and diverse sources that constituted the financial foundation of a spiritual economy focused on the purchase of spiritual "goods" and "services" that were believed to aid the dying and the deceased as they progressed toward their eternal reward.

Yet a surprising element, unmentioned yet quite clear, marks the agreement: the list was *inverted* by the Leisnig community, its many revenues, rents, contributions, and fines now turned toward a common chest that would be used for the "pre-eminently spiritual undertaking [of caring for] the poor and the needy."[45] Monies once devoted to the maintenance of "chapel priests" and their recitation of many masses, daily offices, and rosaries that were believed to help the dead in their movement toward union with God "in heaven" were now redirected to a common chest "on earth" where daily bread could be distributed to the hungry poor.

Supplementing the incomes previously derived from benefices, indulgence sales, and the annuities of the brotherhoods, the agreement noted that each person in the parish should be urged to support the poor with voluntary contributions (i.e., "love gifts") and bequests of property, cash, jewels, or stores designated in a will. Likewise, the agreement asked lay church officials and the pastor to exhort the community to bring offerings of food and other provisions along with coins so that the hungry poor might receive foodstuffs every Sunday. Whenever incomes or donations prove insufficient to meet the needs of the community, the agreement mandated something not found in the Wittenberg Order: an annual tax on every household in the town and parish, "according to ability and means." From those who did not own property but rented or resided freely with relatives or friends in the town and parish, a smaller collection was to be taken. Thus, the agreement established a variety of sources that could be used to support the hungry poor and the needy: ecclesial revenues, voluntary contributions, bequests, and an annual graduated tax. Each citizen, each parishioner, was to contribute to the common welfare of all, especially the neediest: both a religious and civic responsibility.[46]

> The parish assembly solemnly purposes and promises that to the honor of God and the love of our fellow Christians we shall never spare ourselves this trifling annual contribution in view of the fact that hitherto, since time out of mind, both residents and nonresidents throughout our common parish have by many methods and devices been overburdened and fleeced incessantly the year round with exorbitant and intolerable impositions and assessments. By the grace of God these practices have now been restored to the true freedom of the Christian spirit.[47]

Supervision of the common chest was the responsibility of the ten directors elected from the parish worshipping assembly: two nobles, two city council members, three town citizens, and three peasant farmers. To each group of directors, a key was allotted that opened one of the four locks binding the common chest. Thus, four representatives from each of the constituent groups would need to be present for the chest to be opened and the goods therein distributed. Meeting every Sunday, the directors reviewed the books in which were

Figure 6.6. *The parable of the great banquet*, 1562, from a later edition of one of Luther's church postills.

recorded gifts to the common chest, the minutes of every meeting, and the disbursements of every Sunday and weekday when food and other provisions were distributed to the hungry poor and the needy.

Not unlike the Wittenberg Order, the Leisnig Agreement banned begging by panhandlers, monks, "church beggars," students, and

able-bodied persons who refused to work. Yet orphans, poor dependent children, new residents in the city, the temporarily unemployed,
those impoverished thorough circumstance, the sick, and the elderly
were supported by the directors with free disbursements to the unem-
ployable and loans or gifts to those temporarily out of work. Every
Sunday and whenever needed during the days of the ensuing week,
the directors were to distribute food and other provisions from the
common chest to all in need. Likewise, the pastor, sacristan, and male
and female school teachers were to receive an annual stipend and an
appropriate allotment of food so that they might serve the community without worry or distraction. In addition to weekly and annual
disbursements of food, grain was to be purchased and stored "for the
general welfare of our parish" so that in times of scarcity a sufficient
amount would be available for the entire city/parish through purchase,
loans, or free disbursement among those with little or no means. In
effect the agreement established a theologically grounded program of
social welfare, practiced primarily on Sunday, the Lord's day, after the
celebration of the Lord's Supper, in which the Christian worshipping
assembly would see its contributions flowing to hungry neighbors in
need.[48]

Both the Wittenberg and Leisnig orders emerged within six years of
the publication of Luther's Ninety-five Theses, the invitation, extended
in 1517 to university faculty, to discuss the sale of indulgences. In
that relatively short period of time—six years—the movement for the
reform of church and society developed rapidly in Germany and was
embraced rather quickly and enthusiastically by large sections of the
population, by rulers, town and city councils, and clergy. That this was
a movement focused not only on church but also on society is attested
to by the publication of treatises, sermons, and pamphlets that applied
emerging theological perspectives to the pressing social questions and
concerns alive in the towns and cities where "evangelical" reform was
embraced. The Leisnig Agreement was one early "order" that sought
to express an emerging order of life that linked religious and civic concerns. Indeed, the agreement first discloses the community's awareness
of the growing incidence of begging in urban centers that accompanied
food insecurity among those who sought labor in an increasingly mercantile economy. Likewise, the agreement makes clear the community's

awareness of those who need food; these are not unknown strangers "out there," but neighbors who, through chronic sickness, unemployment, physical weakness, or age, could suffer malnourishment.

Second, the agreement suggests that the Leisnig community placed little if any religious or social value in the experience of hunger or poverty. Ancient and medieval Christian voices would laud poor people as the desirable objects of charity for comfortable and wealthy Christians or extol the embrace of voluntary poverty as a privileged form of religious life.[49] Given Luther's criticism of the begging expected in many religious orders, "a crying evil . . . which does so much harm to land and people in soul and property,"[50] it is not surprising that such begging would be forbidden in the agreement. Living with hunger or poverty and its consequence, begging, was not to be accepted as holding any religious value. Hunger and poverty were not to be accepted as "normative," as institutionalized elements of the status quo. Rather, the conditions of hunger and poverty, when possible, were to be remedied: the unemployed are to receive assistance until they can work again or learn a new trade; orphans and impoverished dependent children are to be fed, clothed, and educated at schools funded by the city so that they might, in time, acquire gainful employment; newcomers without work are to be fed and assisted in finding work that will eventually allow them to enter a useful trade. In effect the Leisnig Order carefully set forth and distinguished food relief according to need and ability. While assistance was to be given temporarily until one could work, food and provisions were to be offered regularly and indefinitely to those who, for various reasons, were incapable of labor. Neither legitimate unemployment nor incapacity was to be stigmatized.

Luther visited Leisnig in September 1522 and August 1523 and had cordial relationships with the parish, pastors, and directors of the common chest. What he promoted in his 1520 "Address to the Christian Nobility of the German Nation," a single spiritual estate with no hierarchical ordering, can be discerned in the clear congregational character and claims of the Leisnig assembly. While the Leisnig assembly faced opposition from the abbatial patron of the parish as it began the process of calling its own priest and pastor and using the reformed "evangelical" Mass, it received support from Luther in the form of two publications: "The Right and Power of a Christian Congregation or

Community to Judge All Teaching and to Call, Appoint, and Dismiss
Teachers, Established and Proved from Scripture" (1523) and "Concerning the Ordering of Public Worship" (1523). The first highlighted
the right and responsibility of the baptized to call their own pastoral
leader, while the second offered guidance for the celebration of Christian worship that was both catholic and evangelical.

Prompted by Luther's encouragement and writings, the Leisnig
Agreement revealed, third, an assembly in which responsibility for
appointing pastoral leadership, participating in worship, and directing
relief to the hungry poor was shared among ordinary people, laypeople.
The people appointed and dismissed their pastor; encouraged worship
according to the evangelical reform of the liturgy; claimed rights to
ecclesial lands, buildings, revenues, and rents; established and supported schools with teachers for boys and girls; elected the directors
and set up the administration of their common chest; contributed to
and taxed themselves for the maintenance of their new social welfare
initiative; forbade begging; assisted the unemployed; ordered a par-
ish-wide effort to store ample foodstuffs for times of scarcity; and held
general assemblies three times each year to receive reports and discuss
the effectiveness of their fraternal agreement. "We, the parish assembly," noted the agreement, "by virtue of our universal priesthood, have
always had and should have had full right and authority."[51] Here sacramental vision informed and flowed into civic responsibility, the two
inextricably linked. While Luther had taught the priesthood of all the
baptized three years earlier in his "Address to the Christian Nobility of
the German Nation" and "The Babylonian Captivity of the Church,"
the Leisnig Agreement demonstrated the practical realization of that
teaching.

By claiming the right to receive ecclesial and monastic revenues,
incomes of stunning diversity, and deposit such revenues in the common chest for the common good, the agreement effectively embodied
a fourth reforming impulse: the need to dismantle the spiritualized
economy of the late medieval world and any associations, implied or
explicitly intended, between the offer of money and the promise of
salvation. While the agreement bade the community to disburse an
annual stipend and foodstuffs to the pastor, sacristan, and schoolteach-
ers, it confiscated and then forbade revenues associated with the Mass

or any other service that was celebrated by the church. Indeed, it is not surprising that Luther's concluding exhortation in his "Order of Public Worship," written for the Leisnig assembly, speaks of things flowing freely: "Let everything be done so that the Word may have free course. . . . Again, we profit by nothing as much as by the Word. For the whole Scripture shows that the Word should have free course among Christians."[52] Indeed, once the relationship between "silver coin" and "saving sacrament" had been condemned and then severed, money could flow freely into the common chest that would be used to meet real human needs on this earth and in daily life. As the sacrament and testament of Christ—as the promise of salvation offered indiscriminately and freely "for you and for all"—the reformed Mass could be recognized as the source of Christian social commitment in the world.

In the history of Western Christianity, receiving the wounded Christ—broken body and spilled blood—would be interpreted by some as a sanction for suffering, as nothing more than an accurate description of the reality of human suffering. Spiritualities morbid and self-absorbed would emerge from a eucharistic piety severed from its social dimension. Yet that same action, as Luther made clear, the act of receiving bread in one's hand and drinking wine from a cup, could also become the very act that prompted one to recognize and alleviate the suffering one found in daily life: "When you have partaken of this sacrament . . . you must in turn share the misfortunes of the fellowship . . . Here your heart must go out in love and learn that this is a sacrament of love. As love and support are given you, you in turn must render love and support to Christ in his needy ones . . . You must fight, work, pray."[53] This commitment to the social welfare of the neighbor in need, noted the agreement, is nothing less than a "pre-eminently spiritual undertaking."

7

Greed Is an Unbelieving Scoundrel

In his study of the emergence and diversity of Reformation thought, Alister McGrath notes that while Catholic reform of the sixteenth century focused on clerical education and church administration and the Reformed project was attentive to worship and ethics, Martin Luther and his colleagues were solidly rooted in the reform of theology.[1] McGrath is careful to claim, and rightly so, that these emphases did not preclude reforming initiatives in other areas of church life. Certainly, John Calvin was a reformer of theology and Ignatius Loyola was deeply committed to mission work throughout the world. Yet the claim stands that Luther's reform project began with the theological question of the relationship between God and humanity. It is not surprising, then, to read of the existential anxiety that plagued Luther, the monk, priest, and young professor. Compelled by his anguished search for the merciful face of God, Luther's scholarly research and incessant questioning led him, in time, to what he considered a liberating insight discovered in the letters of Paul: the just shall live by grace, a grace that makes faith itself possible.

Attention to Human Suffering

That this insight, gleaned from Paul, relieved the young monastic priest of his psycho-spiritual *Anfechtung* is well known. As he would exclaim later in life, the very gates of paradise were thrust open to him once he realized the existential import of Paul's assertion that the just live by

115

grace received passively, what Luther would later call "alien righteousness." God offers mercy not damnation. Yet that string of lovely words, "the mercy and grace of God," were not simply a wonderful insight.

One year after Luther's death, a large triptych was installed in the Stadtkirche St. Marien in Wittenberg. Created in the Cranach art studio, the painting portrays the "evangelical" celebration of baptism, the Lord's Supper, and confession. Beneath these three images, there rests a fourth, the "keystone," through which the other three actions were interpreted: on the right stands Luther preaching from a pulpit, arm outstretched as he points to the central

Figure 7.1. Lucas Cranach the Younger, *Altarpiece of the word and sacraments*, 1547, City Church St. Marien, Wittenberg. Photo © Foto Marburg / Art Resource, NY.

figure of the painting: the crucified Christ.[2] In 1518 he would write that the one who deserves to be called a theologian is the one who comprehends the visible and manifest things of God in suffering and the cross. "God wished to be recognized in suffering. . . . God can be found only in suffering and the cross. . . . Therefore, the friends of the cross say that the cross is good and works are evil, for through the cross works are destroyed and the old Adam . . . is crucified. . . . For this reason true theology and recognition of God are in the crucified Christ."[3]

Such an image clearly served a *theological* purpose: Luther insisted that God identifies with and embraces humanity where God is least expected—in humiliation, shame, weakness, suffering, and death. The image and the claim served as a potent critique of the popular image of Christ: the judge who rewards the righteous for their good deeds and punishes the wicked with eternal damnation. The same theological claim was employed to expose the futility of any human effort to move toward God, so enmeshed is the self in its own desires. In the crucified Christ, Luther taught, one recognizes two realities at the same time: the misery of humanity alienated from God and creation and the mercy of God bestowing life, health, and salvation. *Sola gratia* and *solus Christus* flood the sinner with mercy.

The teaching on justification by grace and its corollary, a theology shaped by the crucified Christ, have been interpreted as central elements in Luther's theological project. Consequently, a reform attentive to the suffering of Christ would have great value for constructive theology, theological anthropology, Christology, biblical hermeneutics, and sacramental theology. Indeed, it is not surprising that Cranach painted the reformer pointing to the wide-eyed crucified Christ, a mirror of Luther's own existential suffering and its very antidote. Yet Luther's pointing to the crucified Christ also drew attention to the *human* experience of suffering. There one could see a man stripped and bleeding. After all, it was this first-century Palestinian Jew who experienced torture and cried out, "I thirst." Such a potent image could draw one's attention not only to Christ but also to vulnerable, weak, thirsty human beings. While serving a theological purpose, it could also serve an *anthropological* one by underscoring the perilous nature of human existence. Yes, one sees the suffering Christ, but one can also recognize the many thousands and millions who suffer innocently and unjustly. One could recognize in this Jewish victim, the fate of a conquered and colonized people, indeed, the whole history of human suffering in which the powerful crush the not-so-powerful and the weak.

The theological claim and the artistic image could also hold the awareness of the misery human beings inflict upon each other and the conditions that maintain suffering and deprivation. In the image of the crucified, one could also discern a *social and ethical* dimension. After all Christ was condemned to death by a government official, tortured and crucified by soldiers of the Roman imperial army, and deprived of drink when thirsty. He suffered innocently and unjustly at the hands of an empire that could not tolerate any protest against its imposed "order." In 1517 Luther would criticize the sale of indulgences—a theological, soteriological, and sacramental argument—but also draw attention to the social reality of the poor who were duped by preachers into handing over coins that could have fed a hungry child. Indeed, Luther was mindful of avarice and its remarkable power in human relationships. An insatiable thirst for wealth—manifested visibly in the Renaissance center of Western Christianity and fueled by imperial pillaging of the

New World—were two noticeable instances of corporate grasping that held disastrous consequences for the increasingly landless laborers of early modern Europe, to say nothing of the devastation inflicted upon conquered peoples overseas. Indeed, one could argue that Luther's diagnosis of the human condition—a congenital absorption with oneself and one's many desires apart from grace—could be symbolized by the grasping and "greedy" hand, an individual's hand or an empire's hand: an addiction to "more" for the self or the nation alone, a cunning and cruel exploitation of one's neighbor, the root of social injustice.[4]

For Luther the *incurvatus in se* was not only an individual but also a communal reality discerned in the grocers who charged higher prices in times of scarcity or the church leader who has happy to receive tax revenues from the poor to build a splendid basilica in Rome. The power of grace, as communicated in preaching and the sacraments, was to turn the self-absorbed person or group outward to the other, *curvatus ad extram*, the other who at some point in life would suffer and need assistance. The power of grace, so Luther believed, held the power to transform the greedy and grasping hand into an open and generous one. It is not surprising that throughout his career he had recourse to the liturgical hymn quoted by Paul in his letter to the Philippians: Christ's power was manifested in his service to a suffering humanity, even unto death. The hymn disclosed a Christian assessment of how power is to be exercised "from below" and the paradox that would not let go of the reformer: "Just as [Christ] himself did all things for us, not seeking his own good but ours only—and in this he was most obedient to God—so he desires that we also should set the same example for our neighbors."[5] Where one sees the crucified hand, there one may recognize all those who, in their suffering, beg for bread.

Theology at the Service of Social Teaching

Within two years of the publication of his Ninety-five Theses, Luther, the monk and the priest, was preaching on two kinds of righteousness: the first given freely by God in baptismal washing and the second, flowing from the former, moving the Christian in service toward the neighbor in need.[6] If his theological anthropology first touched the nerve of self-absorption, the assertion of justification by grace drew attention to the spiritual power that enabled one, albeit with great difficulty at times, to move outward in love to other creatures, vulnerable and weak creatures in need of assistance. That "alien" and "proper" righteousness could not be reversed in their order—serving one's neighbor so to please God and gain God's favor or grace—was repeated throughout many written works in a manner so exacting that only the most thickheaded of Germans could miss it. Concerning "proper" or "social" righteousness, Luther wrote: "This [second] righteousness follows the example of Christ in this respect and is transformed into his likeness. It is precisely this that Christ requires."[7] The power of grace mediated through the proclamation of the word, the sacraments of faith, and the Christian assembly could turn one toward life in the world as that life, lived in common with others, is shaped by the economic, political, and social fabric of a cultural epoch. By rejecting the neoplatonic tendencies in Western Christian thought and practice, by denouncing a life lived in the pursuit of the soul's immortality or an other-worldly existence, Luther turned his gaze and that of his followers toward life in *this* world, a world shaped by commerce and law, wealth and poverty, hoarding and hunger.

In just over a year, Luther published what would become three of his most significant works: "To the Christian Nobility of the German Nation Concerning the Reform of the Christian Estate,"[8] "The Babylonian Captivity of the Church,"[9] and "The Freedom of a Christian,"[10] the first articulating an ecclesiology rooted in the sacrament of baptism, the second reforming the Mass and other ecclesial rites, and the third elaborating the Christian's freedom to be a dutiful servant of all. During the same period, he also published works on trade, international commerce, banking practices, state regulation of business, civil insurrection, and governmental authority. While instructing Christians in the christological interpretation of the Gospels,[11] he also preached and wrote on the deleterious effects of usury—inflated interest rates—and the manner in which such a practice insured the growing wealth of the few and the lifelong impoverishment of the many.[12] In 1522, the year in which he published his highly popular prayer book, he also corresponded with the Leisnig assembly and visited the churches in the parish, and he would soon write his preface to the "Ordinance of a Common Chest," bearing his enthusiastic endorsement for the Fraternal Agreement that established one of the earliest Lutheran responses to the hungry poor. In the midst of biblical and devotional texts, there are various letters and sermons that demonstrate the application of theological convictions to pressing social questions, fragments of a theology of social engagement.

While one might agree with the claim that "[Luther's] concern was religious in the first instance and only secondarily economic,"[13] it is hard to ignore the array of works that deal with economic, political, and social questions. Indeed, one need only read the reformer's biblical commentaries to recognize the manner in which he moves from an interpretation of the text in its scriptural or historical context to a discussion of the text's meaning for church or society in sixteenth-century Germany. Thus, in his commentary on Psalm 82, Luther begins with a discussion of God's divine judgment and soon slips into a discourse on the virtues of a German prince, the psalm suddenly speaking about every ruler's duty to enforce just laws, to lend support to orphans, widows, and the poor, and to protect the people against violence and force.[14] "Luther, as an interpreter of Holy Scripture, faced several social and economic problems of his time, in order to denounce and oppose the practice of injustice. In his way, he committed himself to the attempt at the improvement of general life conditions."[15]

What social or economic conditions exacerbated the plight of the hungry poor in sixteenth-century Germany? Individual or corporate lust for profit, he complained, too easily drove out any sense of commitment to the common good.[16] While Luther did not propose a socialist state, he was nonetheless alarmed by the growing gap between the wealthy few who benefited from an unregulated mercantile economy and the many poor who were ignored by the wealthy or governed by unscrupulous rulers who failed to care for their most vulnerable subjects. Where there is no state regulation of business, a regulation that could ensure fair pricing and just trade practices, there is nothing but "a bottomless pit of avarice and wrongdoing."[17] When trading companies actually become monopolies, they can "buy up the entire supply of certain goods . . . in order to have these goods entirely under their own control; they can then fix and raise the price and sell them as dear as they like or can."[18] In contrast to this discriminatory practice, Luther pointed to Joseph who served his ruler by acquiring a substantial supply of food that could be used in times of scarcity to feed a hungry population. The ruler is bound to consider and care for the good of all, including the weakest members of his or her realm, by careful preparations that take into consideration the possibility of both natural and human-made disasters in the future.[19] Indeed, a ruler who governs by reason suffused with wisdom will work to ensure that laws serve the welfare of all who live in his or her realm. Would that it were so, Luther groaned.

Luther quoted the ancient Roman writer Cato, "Simple thieves lie in dungeons and stocks; public thieves walk abroad in gold and silk."[20] While he was aware of trade monopolies that controlled food stores and charged inflated prices—thus effectively denying food to the poor or low-wage laborers—he was also aware of the flow of money from wealthy businesses to kings and princes, a practice that successfully thwarted any governmental regulation of the emerging "global" trading monopolies. If trade monopolies possessed inordinate and unregulated power in controlling goods and services, those who controlled access to money also supported the conditions that could cause or maintain suffering. The practice of usury—making loans at an inflated interest rate—ensured that the poor would remain in perpetual need, their paltry wages spent in paying off the interest but not the principle, a form of economic servitude.[21] This banking practice, denounced throughout the centuries by the church, readily condemned the poor to a

Figure 7.2. Georg Scharffenberg, *Death comes to a usurer*, 1576, from "The Dance of Death."

hand-to-mouth existence and the chronic anxiety that accompanied such a life. This is not to suggest that Luther asked for the abolition of bank loans. Rather, he argued that an exorbitant interest rate should be regulated and dropped to the point where a banker was justly paid and a bank client was not perpetually impoverished. Alas, he lamented, Christ's command, "Do to others as you would have them do to you" (Matt. 7:12), has been evaded and forgotten.[22]

While Luther argued that it was the responsibility of the state, not the church, to propose and enforce just laws and practices that benefit the many, especially the most vulnerable, his own writings on business practices served as a cogent argument for Christian engagement in social and economic questions. While he clearly rejected the notion promoted by some reformers that the state should be governed by "Christian" laws and, in effect, become a theocracy, he nonetheless argued vociferously that Christians must labor with persuasion and genuine love for the abolition of unjust practices or laws that caused or maintained human suffering. In the service of one's neighbor and the common good, a Christian could not stand by in the presence of manifest evil and say or do nothing: "You must fight, work, pray, and—if you cannot do more—have heartfelt sympathy." If one were to tend to the welfare of another human being, such tending and caring would inevitably lead one into the very social conditions that marked one's life with others. Thus, Christians should urge the passage of laws and practices that supported the common good. Grounded in faith and endowed with reason, the Christian is not released from social responsibility. While other reformers would attempt to transform society into a "Christian" state or establish a "holy" community separately, at the margins of society, Luther consistently labored for another position: Christian engagement within society. That commitment to the welfare of the suffering in society can be discerned as early as 1517 when he suggested that it was far better to care for the poor on earth than to buy a quick release into heaven.

In his seminal work on the reinvention of early modern social welfare, Carter Lindberg has helpfully pointed to the theological grounding of Luther's consistent engagement in the social questions of his day. "The secular utility of Luther's theological reorientation," he writes, "is both destructive and constructive."[23] It destroyed or deconstructed the late medieval impulse to care for one's neighbor because such care would prove pleasing in the eyes of God. Luther critiqued the brotherhoods because, in his estimation, they had become centers of communal self-absorption that used their dues to support masses for the dead and violated their charter to assist the needy. They participated in the late medieval spiritual economy that awarded religious "goods and services" to those who could pay or work harder than others. The social value of Luther's theological project was constructive in that "salvation [was] now perceived as the foundation of life rather than the goal and achievement of life, the energy and resources poured into acquiring other-worldly capital [could] be redirected to this-worldly activities."[24] Thus, the Leisnig Agreement to direct church revenues, voluntary donations, and a self-imposed tax to a common chest for the hungry poor was praised as an act of both religious and civic responsibility. The assertion, however, begs the question: Where would Christians find guidance in directing their energies and resources toward human need in a world where it seemed that avarice and unjust practices held sway?

The Trajectory of Word and Sacraments toward the World

"Between the sacraments on the one hand and an ethical life on the other, Luther saw a profound connection."[25] The university professor and German reformer was also a priest and pastor who preached on the biblical texts appointed by the medieval lectionary and presided at the liturgical celebration of the Christian sacraments of baptism and the Lord's Supper. These two responsibilities—theologian and priest—could not be played off each other: the theologian engaged in the pastoral reform of liturgy and sacraments; the pastor and preacher recognized in the Word of God and the celebration of the sacraments a rich source of social and ethical thought. Guided by the central teaching on justification by grace, Luther insisted on the reform of the Mass since the words and actions of this most public and central Christian activity communicated, he argued, the presence of the living Christ to the worshipping assembly.

On the one hand, Luther retained the historic shape of the liturgy: the people gathered with song in the presence of God; listened as the biblical texts were proclaimed and then interpreted for their contemporary meaning; gave thanks to God at table for the gifts of bread and wine; shared and consumed these things as the body and blood of Christ; received God's blessing and were dismissed into the world of daily life. In this regard Luther was not a "destroyer" of received practice since, he noted, the word and the sacraments had been preserved in the church—the Roman Church—albeit with layers of custom and law obscuring their original and simple brightness.[26] On the other hand, Luther promoted a conservative reform of the historic liturgy: the liturgical texts, the biblical readings, and the hymns were translated into the vernacular; the words and actions of the liturgy were pruned of any hint of "sacrifice" offered or "work" accomplished; what seemed to be the simplicity of early Christian practice was promoted; the baptized were encouraged to read the Bible, sing hymns, and study the catechism in

Figure 7.3. *The preaching of the word and the celebration of the sacraments*, 1544, from the "Spiritual Songs of Wittenberg," with a preface by Luther.

their homes so that they would be steeped in the language of Scripture where, Luther claimed, one discovered the perennial spring of reform. Indeed it was that ancient pattern of biblical proclamation set next to preaching, of baptismal washing set next to catechism, of sacramental supper set next to dismissal into daily life that can be traced in his writings from this early period. The christological center of Scripture and preaching was announced in the "Brief Instruction" on the Gospels; the baptismal foundation of the assembly flowed through the "Address to the Christian Nobility"; Christ's meal-testament, shared freely and without discrimination, was set out in the "Blessed Sacrament" and "The Babylonian Captivity."

Indeed, it was the members of the *baptismal assembly* at Leisnig, formed by the proclamation of the *Word of God*, and served food and drink in the *Lord's Supper*, who solemnly pledged themselves to the care and feeding of the hungry poor. It was this baptismal assembly that elected lay Christians as directors of its common chest. It was this assembly, having read and heard the Word of God in their own language that deliberated over the reports, minutes, and effectiveness of their common chest. It was this eucharistic assembly, gathered at the Lord's Supper for bread and cup, which then witnessed the sharing of food and provisions with the hungry poor. Other than Heinrich Kind and Johann Gruner, the parish pastors who may have had access to Luther's writings, the Leisnig assembly was shaped in its "evangelical" identity and social initiatives by the Sunday gathering itself: the biblical texts read and interpreted by their preacher, the hymns sung during the liturgy, the liturgical texts spoken or chanted throughout the Mass, and the sacramental actions of washing, eating, and drinking.

While theologians today may see their work as the advance of knowledge within the precincts of the academy alone and thus only tangentially related to the pastoral commitments and concerns of clergy and laypeople, such a distinction between academy and church was not as clear in the sixteenth century or during the centuries of early Christianity, that period so admired by the reformers. As a theologian and a priest, Luther insisted on the reform of biblical studies, preaching, hymnody, the Mass, and sacramental theology. This was not a momentary but a lifelong pursuit precisely because he recognized the astonishing power of word and action to shape conscience, to "awaken faith in God and love for the neighbor," to cultivate the ethical commitments of Christians who lived in the world. Indeed, most German "evangelicals" in the sixteenth century were more likely to "catch" the current of theological reform by listening to a sermon, singing a hymn, receiving a cup of wine from a married priest, reading a pamphlet, or laughing at a cartoon than by studying a biblical commentary or a theological treatise. Perhaps little has changed. The reformed liturgy and sacraments were the very means, the many media, through which a reform movement rooted in a distinctive theological trajectory would take hold or fail to find a home in the lives of the worshipping assembly. Thus, concerning the relationship between "sacrament" and "ethics," Luther invited the Christian assembly to recognize the social and the economic implications of sharing bread and cup:

> By means of this sacrament, *all self-seeking love is rooted out* and gives
> place to that which seeks the common good of all; and through the

change wrought by love there is one bread, one drink, one body, one community.[27]

See to it that you *give yourself to everyone in fellowship* and by no means exclude anyone in hatred or anger. . . . You must take to heart the infirmities and needs of others as if they were your own. Then offer to others your strength, as if it were their own, just as Christ does for you in the sacrament. This is what it means to change into one another through love, to lose one's own form and *take on that which is common to all.*[28]

Learn that this is a sacrament of love. As love and support are given you, *you in turn must render love and support to Christ in his needy ones.* You must feel with sorrow all the dishonor done to Christ in his holy Word, all the misery of Christendom, all the unjust suffering of the innocent, with which the world is everywhere filled to overflowing. You must fight, work, pray, and—if you cannot do more—have heartfelt sympathy. See, this is what it means to bear in your turn the misfortune and adversity of Christ and his saints. Here the saying of Paul is fulfilled, "Bear one another's burdens, and so fulfill the law of Christ" [Gal. 6:2].[29]

In times past this sacrament was so properly used, and the people were taught to understand this fellowship so well, that *they even gathered food and material goods in the church, and there—as St. Paul writes in I Corinthians 11—distributed among those who were in need.* We have a vestige of this [practice] in the little word "collect" in the mass, which means a general collection, just as a common fund is gathered to be given to the poor.[30]

Here Luther invoked his theological anthropology, both as diagnosis—"self-seeking love"—and as remedy—"the change wrought by [Christ's] love." His theology of Christ the servant appeared: "Offer to others your strength, as if it were their own, just as Christ does for you in the sacrament." He alluded to his Pauline-inspired ecclesiology of *Gemeinde* or fellowship: "There is one bread, one drink, one body, one community. . . . This is what it means to change into one another through love, to lose one's own form and take on that which is common to all." But there was more: he moved from the sacramental Christ and a communing assembly into a world marked by need, misery, misfortune, and adversity. Here participation in the Lord's Supper made one responsible for engaging and alleviating the suffering found in daily life: "You must render love and support to Christ in his needy ones. You must feel with sorrow . . . all the unjust suffering of the innocent. . . . You must fight, work, pray." Indeed, the reformed Mass possessed an ethical trajectory that moves from eating and drinking with Christ to sharing food and drink with the hungry poor: "This sacrament was so properly used, and the people were taught to understand this fellowship so well, that they even gathered food and material goods in the church, and there . . . distributed among those who were in need." In 1519, only two years after he emerged as a public figure committed to reform, Luther had linked sacramental practice and social welfare. His "eucharistic theology" and his "economic ethics" were inseparable: the gathering movement of the Lord's Supper would lead to a sending movement; a communing community was called to attend to human needs and the most vulnerable in daily life.[31]

It is not surprising, then, that the Cranachs juxtaposed the image of the suffering Christ next to the images of the reformed community's liturgical and sacramental celebrations. Again, the juxtaposition served a *theological* purpose: "Do not doubt that you have what the sacrament signifies, that is, be certain that Christ and all his saints are coming to you with all their virtues, sufferings, and mercies, to live, work, and die with you, and that they desire to be wholly yours, having all things in common with you."[32] As the Augsburg Confession would state in 1530, "All ceremonies [of the Mass] should serve the purpose of teaching the people what they need to know about Christ."[33] The ceremonies of the reformed Mass were intended to set forth Christ, the suffering yet risen Christ, coming to the people with mercy. But this was not all. The juxtaposition of the crucified Christ next to the liturgical celebration of the sacraments served a *social* purpose as well: "See to it also that you give yourself to everyone in fellowship and by no means exclude anyone in hatred or anger. . . . You must take to heart the infirmities and needs of others, as if they were your own. . . . Christ has given his holy body for this purpose, that the thing signified by the sacrament—the change wrought by love—may be put into practice."[34] What could have been a "closed" meal practice that benefited the Christian assembly alone, so fiercely critiqued in the brotherhoods, was broken open to human need.[35]

Here Luther linked sacrament and society, Christian worship and social welfare, Christ and culture. The reformed Mass and the celebration of the reformed sacraments were not intended to be a program of social reform that could be imposed upon society or kept by a "holy" community separate from society. For Luther and his colleagues, the proclamation of the Word of God and the celebration of the sacraments *created* the Christian community. In their estimation the Christian assembly was not the author of word and sacraments but the recipient of a prior activity rooted, theologically, in the advance of God toward the community and manifested, sacramentally, through "all the ceremonies" that set forth Christ. From this theological and christological center, mediated sacramentally through human words and actions, there flowed the words and actions that informed Christian presence in the economic, political, and social fabric of society. The Christian community responded to human need in society with the *creation* of public initiatives that focused on the neighbor in need and the common good. Thus, "sacrament" and "service" were understood as two inseparable dimensions of the one advance of God in Christ toward *this* world marked by suffering and misery: "Christ has given his holy body for this purpose, that . . . the change wrought by love may be put into practice." This "body" was to be broken and given away: bread broken in the Lord's Supper, shared in the assembly, distributed among the hungry poor.

The Failure of These Things

While Luther urged Christian assemblies to let their faith become public in works of love and praised the Leisnig assembly for the "structured" generosity spelled out in its Fraternal Agreement, he also recognized the struggle entailed in the mandate to remain socially engaged. It would have been easier to consider the Christian assembly a "holy" community separate from the world. It would have been possible, though doomed to failure so he believed, to transform society into a Christian utopia, an experiment that emerged briefly in Geneva and parts of the American colonies. He and his colleagues insisted that the gospel could not become public law enforced with punitive measures; the two, gospel and law, would be disastrously confused and return the church to the very situation that prompted theological reform. Since Luther understood human beings as continually living in the struggle between the *incurvatus in se* and the *curvatus ad extram*, no humanly constructed social initiative, as brilliant or helpful as it might be, could claim an ultimate loyalty or be equated with the kingdom of God. As he noted in the explanation to the Lord's Prayer, "God's kingdom comes on its own without our prayer, but we ask in this prayer that it may come to us also."[36] While Christians are called to serve God and the advent of God's kingdom in this world and while they enjoy the use of both faith and reason in the promotion of social initiatives that benefit the common good, they only deal in destructive fantasies when they equate their projects with God's kingdom. In Luther's estimation, no project, cause, or idea, created and promoted by humans marked with limited knowledge and wisdom, could ask for one's fundamental loyalty. No cause, project, or idea could transform society into the kingdom of God. By virtue of one's baptism, a Christian is called to serve that kingdom, which is God's alone, in this world. Yet one could not "build" that kingdom in this world. Such a claim would be to risk idolatry, the worship of a false god.

Rejecting an idealistic appraisal of both human beings and their theologically inspired social initiatives, Luther held what he believed was a more realistic assessment of ecclesial and social reform: there will be advances and there will be failure. "Dear God, what misery I beheld! The ordinary person, especially in the villages, knows absolutely nothing about the Christian faith, and unfortunately many pastors are completely unskilled and incompetent teachers. Yet supposedly they all bear the name Christian, are baptized, and received the holy sacrament, even though they do not know the Lord's Prayer."[37]

Five years after he published his preface to the Leisnig Agreement, Luther made an official visitation of the Saxon congregations where the reform had been received. What he encountered led him to speak of a "deplorable" and "wretched deprivation" throughout the region. So frustrated was he with the pace and depth of reform and the lack of Christian teaching among the people that he called them *pagani*, pagans.[38] Pastors and bishops fared no better for their "shameful neglect" of the people. Clearly, the struggle to advance the reform project throughout Germany could fail. Shallow preaching and teaching, when combined with impoverished liturgical practice, would leave the people deprived of the sources of faith and love. Where the first collapses, the second disappears.

Luther recognized that Christians might regularly participate in the Mass but fail to grasp its benefits and risks:

> There are those, indeed, who would gladly share in the profits but not in the costs. That is, they like to hear that in this sacrament the help, fellowship, and support of all the saints are promised and given to them. But they are unwilling in their turn to belong also to this fellowship. They will not help the poor, put up with sinners, care for the sorrowing, suffer with the suffering, intercede for others, defend the truth, and at the risk of [their own] life, property, and honor seek the betterment of the church and of all Christians. They are unwilling because they fear the world. They do not want to have to suffer disfavor, harm, shame, or death, although it is God's will that they be thus driven—driven for the sake of the truth and of their neighbors—to desire the great grace and

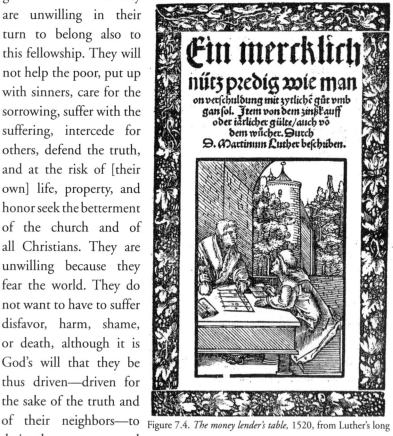

Figure 7.4. *The money lender's table,* 1520, from Luther's long sermon on usury.

strength of this sacrament. They are self-seeking persons, whom this sacrament does not benefit.[39]

Without understanding, the celebration of the sacraments in the Christian assembly would be received with an ignorance that could easily lead to superstition and thoughts of magic. Where preaching and teaching were weak, the proper theological orientation for life in the world would be absent. When, in the face of human suffering and the risk entailed to ameliorate such suffering, apathy and indolence prevailed, the word and the sacraments would not find a receptive home. When "sacraments do not benefit," the problem is not in the sacrament but in either the preaching and teaching that fails to "awaken faith" to the sacrament's "great grace and strength" or human resistance to what the sacrament asks of those who receive it: help the poor, put up with sinners, care for the sorrowing, suffer with the suffering, intercede for others, defend the truth, and seek the betterment of all.

While Luther would claim that the resurgence of the "holy gospel" in his time had revealed the "works of darkness" (i.e., financial evils) and that some merchants, in fact, had been convicted of their sinful business practices and turned away from them, he also recognized that his proposals for economic reform might be scorned and ignored:

I suppose that my writing will be quite in vain, because the mischief has gone so far and has completely gotten the upper hand in all lands; and because those who understand the gospel are probably able in such easy, external things to judge for themselves what is fair and what is not, on the basis of their own consciences. Nevertheless, I have been asked and urged to touch upon these financial evils and expose some of them so that, even though the majority may not wish to do right, at least some people—however few they are—may be delivered from the gaping jaws of avarice. For it must be that among the merchants, as among other people, there are some who belong to Christ and would rather be poor with God than rich with the devil, as Psalm 37[:16] says, "It is better for the righteous to have a little than to have the great possessions of the wicked."[40]

Compelled to speak out on behalf of the poor who suffered the discriminatory practices of unscrupulous merchants, Luther also knew that the diets seemed to have limited power to curb or regulate the growing power of trade monopolies and the increasingly usurious practices of the banks.[41] Business and banking lobbyists were quite effective in the use of bribes to sway the favor of political leaders and elections. Merchants would toss his advice to the winds, he noted, and simply remain as they were.[42] Neither the gospel nor reason could prove convincing where avarice prompted merchants to charge the highest price they could for food and drink. Cognizant of the economic and social conditions that produced or maintained the suffering of the hungry poor, Luther recognized the remarkable power found in the drive to gain capital as well as the seeming ineffectiveness of his own protest against the promoters of an economic system that seemed less and less interested in directing its "energies and resources" toward the common good.

Such was the case in Leisnig. Although the Fraternal Agreement established a common chest for the hungry poor and directed the election of administrators of the community's charity and taxes, the city council was unwilling to hand over its right to the ecclesial endowments and bequests that had been seized from "Roman" churches and monasteries. While Luther had enthusiastically endorsed the Fraternal Agreement as an early "evangelical" experiment in social welfare reform, he concluded his preface with a note of caution if not resignation: "If anyone does not care to follow these suggestions, and in so doing quench his greed, I wash my hands of him. Well do I know that few will accept such advice. I am content if only one or two follow me, or would at least like to follow me. The world must remain the world, and Satan its prince. I have done what I can, and what I am in duty bound to do. God help us all to do what is right and to stand firm. Amen."

Indeed, the city council did not accept his advice: not a pfennig would be given to the common chest without the express approval of the elector. In the summer of 1523, Luther visited the city to urge the council to make funds available to the common chest. The council members remained steadfast in their resistance to his pleading. The situation worsened to the point that, in the following year, Luther complained that the town's preacher would have to leave because he had no funds with which to buy food.[43] The man suffered from sheer hunger.

Throughout these writings Luther clearly acknowledged that reform could fail. Merchants, rulers, bishops, teachers, pastors, civic administrators, the hungry poor, laborers, theologians—indeed all people—were susceptible to misunderstanding, self-absorption, pride, fear, and the "gaping jaws of avarice." Through the simple observation of human relationships, one could find adequate grounds to despair of any change in human consciousness or behavior. As a student and teacher of the Bible, Luther knew that the prophets who called for the reform of the people and their leaders frequently met with failure if not death. Indeed, the central figure in the Christian story was silenced, so it seemed, by a tragic and public end, abandoned by most of his followers and mocked as a failed "king." This Luther knew as well. While he was utterly convinced of the truth revealed in his study of the Pauline writings—the just shall live by grace through faith—and steadfastly embraced the *sola gratia* in the midst of his own debilitating bouts with depression, he also recognized that the Word of God falls on rocky and unreceptive soil: "Many possess it, but do not believe in it or act by it."[44] That Christians who possessed the Word of God would "act by it" remained an open and troubling question.

Fragments of a Social Ethic

As early as 1517 Luther was aware of the hungry poor who populated the towns and cities of Germany. In that context his promotion of the Pauline teaching on "justification by grace alone" served both theological and social purposes. The human being could do nothing to gain God's favor: all humans—the wealthy as well as the hungry poor, the professor as well as the peasant—were caught in the force field of the *incurvatus in se*. Any attempt to work one's way up and out of this world, as the spiritual economy of late medieval Christianity suggested, was futile. Only an external and prior action, the advance of a merciful God toward humanity, revealed in Jesus Christ and mediated through word and sacraments, could arrest the power of that inward curve toward self-absorption and thus pull one outward toward God and other creatures. In effect this reorientation of spiritual

power and affections criticized an ancient patronage system that had
perdured throughout the late Middle Ages and the Renaissance: God
the "patron" would favor with "benefits" those who were capable of
offering a "gift." It is little wonder that Luther consistently spoke of
"gift" and "treasure," no longer an offering or "sacrifice" made to God
with the expectation of receiving "favor," but rather an unexpected,
free, and "unmerited" bestowal of "goods" independent of one's capacity to be productive or useful in a mercantile economy, spiritual or
secular.

By eliminating any need to "work out one's salvation with trem-
bling and fear"—since the favor of God was bestowed permanently on
a squalling infant, the least "productive" member of any economy—
the Christian was free to consider this world as the appropriate arena
for action, what Luther spoke of as one's service to the neighbor in
need. As he noted in his address "To the Christian Nobility of the German Nation," baptism bestows "priesthood" upon the Christian but a
"priesthood" of service to others exercised in the world of daily life, a
theological conviction that contained a social dimension.[45] Guided by
faith, rather than superstition, the Christian was free to attend to real
human need simply because to do so benefited the other and participated in the expansion of "life, health, and salvation" into all spheres
of life.

"A Christian is the servant of all and made subject to all. Insofar
as he is free he does no works, but insofar as he is a servant he does all
kinds of works."[46] Guided by faith and the knowledge that he or she
is the recipient of God's mercy, the Christian exercises faith actively
through works of love. "In this way the strong member may serve the
weaker. . . . Each caring for and working for the other, bearing one
another's burdens and so fulfilling the law of Christ [Gal. 6:2]. This is
a truly Christian life."[47]

While claiming that baptism and faith thrust the Christian into a
life of service in this world, rather than as preparation and plea for the
life of the world to come, Luther recognized that the strong frequently
overpower if not crush the weak. The call to recognize the "weaker"
member and serve that person or group was not a calling "natural" to
human beings. Indeed, it was a calling that would shrivel up unless

Figure 7.5. *The parable of the good Samaritan*, 1544, from a commentary by Luther on the Epistles and Gospels appointed for the Sundays from Easter to the beginning of Advent.

constantly nourished through the "means of grace"—the preaching of the Word of God and the celebration of the sacraments—and life in the Christian assembly.

Luther recognized in the Bible a *Spiegel* of his own time, a mirror that contained invitations and instructions for responding to the hungry poor in sixteenth-century Germany. Formation in these invitations and instructions was one of the primary functions of preaching and teaching. Scripture taught that what God has given graciously through the agency of creation—food and drink—is to be shared according to human need. Indeed, the meal of Christians, the Lord's Supper, could be celebrated according to the pattern of the early Christian community: some bread and some wine set aside for the Mass and the rest distributed among the hungry poor, the one Christian meal now opened to all those in need.

Such a desire to care for the "weaker" members of society could take the form of a "structured" generosity, a common chest, a Christian and a civic response to the widow, the indigent, and the orphan. Here "treasure" would be offered freely in support of the common good.

And so theological vision and sacramental practice inspired social teaching, which in turn created a pastoral and civic response to human need. Theology or social teaching: was one more important than the other? While claiming the priority of theology, of "alien" righteousness, of Christ as gift, of baptism as prior claim, of Mass as testament, one still might answer the question with another. *Which is more important: breathing out or breathing in?* For with social ethics, "proper" righteousness, Christ as example, baptism as worldly priesthood, and Mass as preparation for service, the advance of grace throughout every dimension of human existence could flow freely.

To say the least, there is no systematic treatment of Christian response to the hungry poor in Luther's writings. There are only fragments that can be culled and then placed next to each other: a baptized assembly, formed in portions of an ancient book and the fragment of a Mediterranean supper, responding to real human need, indeed, the most fundamental human need.

Luther wrote that Greed is a disobedient and unbelieving scoundrel,[48] a ravenous consumption of what rightly belongs to all. The Christians at Leisnig said something else: We feed the hungry poor so that no one need ever beg or cry out.[49] Their words are both memory and challenge in a world where the open hands of the many wait to be filled with a fragment of bread, in a world where the skeptical voice of the prophet asks, "Who benefits from keeping the hungry poor both hungry and poor?"

NOTES

Chapter 1. Baskets Filled with Fragments

1. Cf. Matt. 14:13-21; Luke 9:10-17; John 6:1-13.

2. Exodus 16:1-36 narrates God's provision of manna and quail, perhaps two separate and earlier traditions combined by the editor of Exodus.

3. See Ezek. 34:2-5 and Zech. 11:4-17.

4. See Ps. 23:1; Isa. 65:10; Ezek. 34:15.

5. On the Galilean fishing industry and the role of fish in peasant life, see K. C. Hanson and Douglas Oakman, *Palestine in the Time of Jesus: Social Structures and Social Conflicts* (Minneapolis: Fortress Press, 1998), 106–10. On bread and fish as symbolic yet culturally "open" food in emerging Jewish Christianity, see Graydon Snyder, *Inculturation of the Jesus Tradition: The Impact of Jesus on Jewish and Roman Cultures* (Harrisburg, Pa.: Trinity, 1999), 148–50. "The simple meal of Christians democratized the Greco-Roman class system. Luxurious banquets, with their ranking of clients, were no longer acceptable" (150).

6. "Because of the frequency of this feeding narrative (six times in the four Gospels) and the frequency of artistic representations of the feeding and/or the related Agape, the story must be taken seriously as data for meals in the early church." Snyder, *Inculturation*, 161.

7. The occupation of Palestine by the Roman imperial army was not only a political problem for Palestinian Jews, it was also a theological one: God was the "ruler" who had given God's land to the chosen people as their dwelling place and for their livelihood. The two dimensions, political and theological, could not and cannot be separated. Thus, blessing God over bread or wine or fish as the "ruler" or "king" of the universe was not only a theological affirmation but also a subversive protest in the context of Roman occupation: there could be only *one* "ruler," the shepherd of Israel; not that other ruler, who claimed to control the land, its fields, orchards, rivers, and lakes.

8. On patronage in Roman Palestine, see Hanson and Oakman, *Palestine*, 70–86. "The urban elites of Judah/Judea sought out the backing

of a series of imperial states because the patronage of these foreign states provided protection . . . access to power . . . religious control . . . and inducement (control of land and economic resources). . . . The peasantry, on the other hand, had little or nothing to gain from these shifting alliances" (87).

9. Drawn from anthropological research the distinction between "pure" and "impure" not only refers to *physical* purity or impurity (e.g., a living, healthy body versus a dead, decaying body) but also culturally constructed notions of *social* purity or impurity (e.g., a virgin, the gainfully employed versus a prostitute, someone on the dole) and *religious* purity or impurity (e.g., an observant Jew or "faithful" Christian versus a nonobservant Jew or a "nominal" Christian). On the function of purity and impurity in Roman Palestine, see Marcus Borg, *Jesus: A New Vision: Spirit, Culture, and the Life of Discipleship* (San Francisco: HarperSanFrancisco, 1987), 79–96; John Dominic Crossan, *Jesus: A Revolutionary Biography* (San Francisco: HarperSanFrancisco, 1994), 75–101; Gordon Lathrop, *Holy People: A Liturgical Ecclesiology* (Minneapolis: Fortress Press, 1999), 183–97.

10. "The term 'sinners' referred to an identifiable *social* group, just as the term 'righteous' did: those who did not follow the ways of the fathers as spelled out by the Torah wisdom of the sages . . . [this social group] included the notoriously wicked . . . as well as members of certain occupational groups, membership in which made one as a 'non-Jew.' " Borg, *Jesus*, 92, emphasis mine. In the Gospels Jesus is mocked as one who "welcomes sinners and eats with them." Jesus welcomes and eats with social outcasts, a group that "included many of the poor" (132).

11. Walter Brueggemann argues that Jesus stood within the line of prophets, beginning with Moses, who resisted the "royal" or monarchical consciousness and its corollary, a socially stratified society with the narrow concentration of economic, political, and social power at the pinnacle. See his *The Prophetic Imagination*, 2nd ed. (Minneapolis: Fortress Press, 2001), especially 81–113. In the context of Roman occupation, the Passover memory of freedom from servitude, provision of food for all people, and an unmediated relationship between God and the people served as a vital alternative and a critique of Roman and Judean "elite" control of the temple and the image of God communi-

cated there. See also Douglas Oakman, "The Lord's Prayer in Social Perspective," *Authenticating the Words of Jesus*, ed. Bruce Chilton and Craig Evans (Leiden: Brill, 1999), 137–86.

12. Jesus' conflict with those who controlled the temple and its practices has gained increasing prominence as scholars recognize his protest as one of the probable causes for his arrest and subsequent crucifixion. On the significance of Jesus' demonstration against temple practice, see Borg, *Jesus*, 172–89; Hanson and Oakman, *Palestine*, 131–59, especially 155–56. The story also gained new prominence in the sixteenth century as a justification for criticism of church practices, the reformers placing themselves with Jesus against the "temple priests," the Roman hierarchy.

13. See Isa. 56:6-8; Matt. 8:11; Luke 13:29; also Mark 8:1-9, perhaps a Markan device to demonstrate the expansion of the Jesus/early Christian movement among other people, the number seven symbolic of the people or nations surrounding Israel.

14. Consider the interpretation of Jesus' last days in Marcus Borg and John Dominic Crossan, *The Last Week: A Day-by-Day Account of Jesus's Final Week in Jerusalem* (San Francisco: HarperSanFrancisco, 2006).

15. While corrected by later studies, see Adalbert Hamman, *Vie liturgique et vie sociale: repas des pauvres, diaconie et diaconat, agape et repas de charité offrande dans l'antiquité chrétienne* (Paris: Desclée, 1968), 11–66, 155–230; "Agape," *Encyclopedia of Early Christianity*, ed. Everett Ferguson (New York: Garland, 1997), 16–17; Snyder, *Inculturation*, 171–74.

16. On the different types of prophets found in the Bible, see Gail Ramshaw, *Treasures Old and New: Images in the Lectionary* (Minneapolis: Fortress Press, 2002), 326–27.

17. Hanson and Oakman, *Palestine*, 154.

18. John Dominic Crossan claims that open eating and free healing were the two central actions of Jesus and the early Jesus movement. These two parabolic and reciprocal prophetic actions, he argues, enacted the reign of God "here and now." See his *The Essential Jesus: Original Sayings and Earliest Images* (Edison: Castle, 1998), 9–13.

Chapter 2. The Church Fishes for Wealth

1. Alister McGrath, *Reformation Thought: An Introduction* (Oxford: Blackwell, 1999), 5–11.

2. Oswald Bayer, "Martin Luther," *The Reformation Theologians*, ed. Carter Lindberg (Oxford: Blackwell, 2002), 51–66; Martin Brecht, *Martin Luther: His Road to Reformation, 1483-1521*, trans. James L. Schaaf (Philadelphia: Fortress Press, 1985), 46-82; Eric W. Gritsch, *A History of Lutheranism* (Minneapolis: Fortress Press, 2002), 6–11; Peter Manns, *Martin Luther* (New York: Crossroad, 1982), 25–30, 50–62; Martin Marty, *Martin Luther* (New York: Viking Penguin, 2004), 17–51; Heiko Oberman, *Luther: Man between God and the Devil*, trans. Eileen Walliser-Schwarzbart (New York: Image Doubleday, 1992), 124–29.

3. *D. Martini Lutheri Opera Latina varii argumenti* (Frankfurt and Erlangen: Jung et Filii, 1865–73), 1:273, as quoted in Oberman, *Luther*, 188.

4. Ibid.

5. Luther's publication of his "Disputation on the Power and Efficacy of Indulgences" (commonly called the Ninety-five Theses) was not his first objection to the practice. In his lectures on the Psalms, dating from 1514, he noted the deleterious effects of indulgences: "There is much worship of God everywhere, but it is only going through the motions, with no love and spirit, and there are very few with any fervor. And all this happens because we think we are something and are doing enough. Consequently we try nothing, and we hold to no strong emotion, and we do much to ease the way to heaven, by means of indulgences, by means of easy doctrines, feeling that one sigh is enough." *First Lectures on the Psalms* [Psalms 1–75], *Luther's Works* 10 (hereafter *LW*], ed. Jaroslav Pelikan et al. (St. Louis: Concordia, 1974), 3.

6. When he translated the New Testament into Latin, the vernacular language of the fourth-century Western empire, Jerome used the term *poenitentiam agite* as an equivalent of the original Greek *metanoiete*. The Latin term, however, can be readily translated as "[you must] do penance," rather than "turn toward" or "turn around." As a biblical scholar versed in Hebrew and Greek as well as Latin and German, Luther could discern *the difference in meaning* the two terms possessed.

7. *LW* 31:31.

8. The chief heraldic symbol of the bishop of Rome, successor of Peter, remains two crossed keys, first seen in the dome of the Arian baptistery in Ravenna where an early sixth-century mosaic shows Peter holding keys in his hand. With greater visual power the connection between Peter, the bishop of Rome, and the power of the keys is made in the six-foot-high inscription found in the interior band at the base of the dome of the Basilica of St. Peter in the Vatican: TU ES PETRUS ET SUPER HANC PETRAM AEDIFICABO ECCLESIAM MEAM ET TIBI DABO CLAVES REGNI CAELORUM ("You are Rock, and on this rock I will build my church, and I will give to you the keys of the kingdom of heaven").

9. *LW* 31:31.

10. *LW* 31:28.

11. *LW* 31:31.

12. *LW* 31:28.

13. Lee Wandel, "Social Welfare," *The Oxford Encyclopedia of the Reformation*, ed. Hans Hillerbrand (New York: Oxford University Press, 1996), 4:77.

14. Catharina Lis and Hugo Soly, *Poverty and Capitalism in Pre-Industrial Europe* (Atlantic Highlands: Humanities, 1979), 53–96. As poor peasants were freed from serfdom, the negligible form of economic protection found in a feudal economy—greater indebtedness to a vassal or lord—was lost. Many artisans and field workers who moved to cities in search of economic opportunity became a part of the urban poor. Wandel suggests that as much as 25 percent of the population was continually underfed. On the assessment of poverty in late medieval and early modern Europe, see *Aspects of Poverty in Early Modern Europe*, ed. Thomas Riis (Alphen aan den Rijn: Sijthoff, 1981); *Aspects of Poverty in Early Modern Europe II: Les réactions des pauvres à la pauvreté*, ed. Thomas Riis (Odense: Odense University Press, 1986); Carter Lindberg, *Beyond Charity: Reformation Initiatives for the Poor* (Minneapolis: Fortress Press, 1993), 17–67; Friedrich Luetge, "The Fourteenth and Fifteenth Centuries in Social and Economic History," *Pre-Reformation Germany*, ed. Gerald Strauss (New York: Harper & Row, 1972), 316–79; Michael Mollat, *The Poor in the Middle Ages*, trans. Arthur Goldhammer (New Haven: Yale University Press, 1986); Merry Wiesner, "Making Ends Meet: The Working Poor

in Early Modern Europe," *Pietas et Societas: New Trends in Reformation Social History*, ed. Kyle Sessions and Phillip Bebb (Kirksville: Sixteenth Century Journal Publishers, 1985), 79–88.

15. Wandel, "Social Welfare," 77.

16. *LW* 31:29.

17. *LW* 31:29.

18. *LW* 31:30.

19. *LW* 31:33.

20. Peter Matheson, *The Imaginative World of the Reformation* (Minneapolis: Fortress Press, 2001), 20.

21. *LW* 31:31.

22. The understanding of grace as a transforming power that fashions or remolds human beings was articulated by Augustine of Hippo in the fifth century. His theology of grace wielded considerable influence in the medieval theology of grace as a sanctifying power that enabled one to grow more and more in love of God and others, to grow in holiness. In this understanding grace primarily transforms the person and secondarily forgives the person of sin. Luther would break with this theology of grace. He would assert that grace is primarily the mercy of God that forgives the sin of people. Luther became deeply suspicious of the notion of grace as a transforming power because it could not guarantee that a Christian would be acceptable to God. How much transformation is needed *in this life* to make one "acceptable" to God on the day of judgment? Consequently, grace as transforming power became a secondary if not negligible emphasis in Luther's thought. The dialectic between forgiveness and sin in human life dominated; thus, his understanding of the Christian as always *simul iustus et peccator*, at the same time justified by God's grace and yet a sinner, emerged.

23. The distinction between the two is significant. By the sixteenth century Western Christianity celebrated seven sacraments—baptism, confirmation, eucharist, penance, marriage, holy orders, and extreme unction (the last rites of the dying that included confession and Communion)—each one, so the church affirmed, instituted or countenanced by Christ. At the same time numerous "sacramentals"— extensions of the sacraments—had developed. These included words (prayers, blessings, private reading of Scripture), actions (the sign of the cross, receiving ashes, blessing oneself with holy water, following

the stations of the cross, making a pilgrimage to a shrine or church), and the use of blessed objects (cross, rosary, palms). That late medieval Christians could easily distinguish between the two remains an open question. That some people and their priests viewed both sacraments and sacramentals magically or superstitiously has been recognized by both Protestant and Roman Catholic scholars in the last fifty years.

24. Josef Lortz, *The Reformation in Germany*, trans. Ronald Walls (New York: Herder & Herder, 1968), 1:109–43, emphasis mine.

25. Lindberg, *Beyond Charity*, 95.

26. *LW* 31:31.

27. "The Babylonian Captivity of the Church," *LW* 36:35.

28. The English word *communion* is derived from Latin *communio* and *communere*, that is, a *sharing* of services or gifts.

29. Lester Little, *Liberty, Charity, Fraternity: Lay Religious Confraternities at Bergamo in the Age of the Commune* (Northampton: Smith College, 1988), 97, as quoted in Lindberg, *Beyond Charity*, 30.

30. This is not to say that many or some Christians of means crassly viewed the peasant or the urban poor as subhuman. The late medieval religious imagination was influenced by the judgment scene in which the Son of Man identifies himself with the hungry and the thirsty (Matt. 25:31-46), the Benedictine monastic practice of recognizing each guest or stranger as Christ, and the powerful figure of Francis of Assisi and his followers who insisted that care for the poor was care for Christ himself. In the context of the search for salvation in the late Middle Ages, offering charity to the hungry and the poor was approved and promoted by the church as a means of helping *the giver of charity* receive a merciful judgment from God. A modest investment in this life could lead to a remarkable return in the life to come.

3. Buying Spiritual Goods and Services

1. See the title page woodcut of Hans Sachs' *Die Wittenbergisch Nachtigall* (1523) in Peter Matheson, *The Imaginative World of the Reformation* (Minneapolis: Fortress Press, 2001), 31–33.

2. "Heidelberg Disputation," in Timothy F. Lull, ed., *Martin Luther's Basic Theological Writings*, 1st ed. (Minneapolis: Fortress Press, 1989), 30.

3. Ibid., 43.

4. Ibid., 43–44.

5. Ibid., 46. Feminist Christian theologians have argued recently and, at times, persuasively, that an almost exclusive emphasis in Lutheran theology on God's embrace of suffering, passivity before grace, and the crucifixion of Jesus can be received as symbols of oppression by women and others who are accorded secondary status or "passive" roles in society. When suffering or passivity are emphasized as "normative" religious postures within a patriarchal culture and/or religion, women and others can be socialized into the acceptance of passive suffering even when such passivity (e.g., at the hands of an abusive spouse or a misogynist corporation) jeopardizes life or the means to support life. The claim that God embraces suffering does not necessarily lead one to conclude that God is interested in the relief of suffering. I have suggested that the "embrace of suffering" was and is useful theologically because it claims that God is not aloof from but attentive to any form of human suffering. Without the corresponding emphasis on the *alleviation* of suffering, on life, on resurrections major and minor, however, crucifixion, suffering, and passivity can, all too easily, support less than life, diminishment, even death. See Gail Ramshaw, *Under the Tree of Life: The Religion of a Feminist Christian* (Akron, Ohio: OSL Publications, 2003), 69–120, in particular, 101–14.

6. Lull, *Luther's Basic Writings*, 46–47; emphasis mine.

7. Ibid., 48.

8. "Two Kinds of Righteousness," in ibid., 155.

9. Ibid.

10. Luther never used the term "Christian anthropology," a category of more recent vintage. "Christian anthropology" refers to one's understanding of humanity and the human condition from a Christian perspective.

11. *LW* 25:245. Luther's understanding of humanity's inward turn emerged in his lectures on the Letter of Paul to the Romans, given in 1515–16 at Wittenberg.

12. Luther's understanding of the human condition and the work of Christ is set forth poetically in his hymn paraphrase of Psalm 46, "A Mighty Fortress Is Our God." Christ is interpreted as the liberator of humanity from the forces of evil; thus, the image of "Christus Victor" comes to the fore. This emphasis in Christology can be traced to the

writer-editor of the Gospel of John (Luther's favorite Gospel) and the early Christian bishop Irenaeus of Lyons. See Justo González, *Christian Thought Revisited: Three Types of Theology*, rev. ed. (Maryknoll: Orbis, 1999), 33–47, 107–21. For a Lutheran perspective rooted in yet critical of liberation theology, see Walter Altmann, "The Cross," in *Luther and Liberation: A Latin American Perspective*, trans. Mary Solberg (Minneapolis: Fortress Press, 1992), 13–25.

13. *LW* 25:291. Luther employs Paul's Adam/first human–Christ/second human typology as symbols of the human turned inward on the self, deceit, and death and the human turned outward toward God and others, truth, and life.

14. Lull, *Luther's Basic Writings*, 157.

15. Ibid., 156. While Luther would claim that "alien righteousness" does make progress throughout a Christian's life and is not perfected until death, that assertion needs to be held within his insistence that the Christian remains *simul iustus et peccator* throughout life. Here he would reinforce the dialectical character of his theology: the Christian and the Christian community lives within the constant struggle, the dialectical pull, between the force field of sin (being turned inward on the self) and that of grace (being turned outward in faith toward God and love toward others).

16. Ibid.

17. Sammeli Juntunen, Tuomo Mannermaa, Simo Puera, Antti Raunio, and Risto Saarinen—Luther scholars at the University of Helsinki—have argued that the center of Luther's understanding of salvation is union with Christ, a union that shares some commonalities with the Eastern Orthodox conception of entering into the divine life. In the Finnish view Christ is the very "righteousness of God" offered graciously by God to the baptized sinner. Baptism initiates one into participation in the divine, grace-filled life of God. Wary of using ontological categories to describe the phenomenon of salvation, other Luther scholars (notably German ones and those they have influenced, so the Finns argue) have been critical of the Finnish interpretation and would argue against any ontological conceptualization of "union with Christ," preferring instead an emphasis on the forensic justification of the sinner, that is, the *declaration* of forgiveness proclaimed to humanity. See *Union with Christ: The New Finnish Interpretation of Luther*, ed.

Carl Braaten and Robert Jenson (Grand Rapids: Eerdmans, 1998).

18. Jared Wicks, *Luther and His Spiritual Legacy*, Theology and Life Series 7 (Wilmington: Glazier, 1983), 139.

19. "To the Christian Nobility of the German Nation Concerning the Reform of the Christian Estate," *LW* 44:115–217.

20. Lull, *Luther's Basic Writings*, 156.

21. Carter Lindberg, *Beyond Charity*, 97.

22. Lull, *Luther's Basic Writings*, 157.

23. Ibid., 156.

24. Rodney Stark, *The Rise of Christianity: How the Obscure, Marginal Jesus Movement Became the Dominant Religious Force in the Western World in a Few Centuries* (San Francisco: HarperSanFrancisco, 1997), 211.

25. Clearly, the ancient Mediterranean world was filled with stories about gods and goddesses who took human form in order to be seen by humans. Yet the story of a god or goddess who would abandon his or her powers and take human form to *serve humanity unto death* is difficult to find.

26. Stark, *Rise of Christianity*, 212.

27. The artistic juxtaposition of events from the life of Christ with events from the life of the pope and the papal curia was vividly portrayed in Lucas Cranach's *Passional Christi et Antichristi* of 1521. See Josef Koerner, *The Reformation of the Image* (Chicago: University of Chicago Press, 2004), 104–36; R. W. Scribner, *For the Sake of Simple Folk: Popular Propaganda for the German Reformation* (Oxford: Clarendon, 1984, 1991), 148–89.

28. Here I am referring to the "broken myth" discussed by Paul Tillich in *Dynamics of Faith* (New York: Harper, 1957), 52–54. In his reflection on the biblical use of the "broken myth," Gordon Lathrop writes that "the old is maintained; yet, by means of juxtaposition and metaphor, the old is made to speak the new." *Holy Things: A Liturgical Theology* (Minneapolis: Fortress Press, 1993), 27. The "old" is maintained ("God is powerful"), yet by means of juxtaposition ("God is revealed as servant to humanity," God is revealed in the death of the "son of God"), the old ("God is powerful") is made to speak the new ("God's power is exercised in service among and to humanity, especially the most vulnerable and anxious of humans").

29. Lull, *Luther's Basic Writings*, 159.

30. Ibid., 160–61.

31. Ibid., 158; emphasis mine.

32. Ibid., 106.

33. Ibid., 107.

34. Thomas à Kempis, *The Imitation of Christ* (Milwaukee: Bruce, 1949), 3.

35. Thus, Luther and his colleagues would steadfastly resist the temptation to construct a society ruled by religious leaders who would use the Bible as a book of civil law: gospel would be transformed into civic requirement and the teaching on justification by grace would be turned on its head. The temptation, nonetheless, has always been present throughout the history of Christianity and remains a goal for some Christian communities in North America.

36. On the centrality of justification by grace in Luther's ethics, see Paul Althaus, *The Ethics of Martin Luther*, trans. Robert Schultz (Philadelphia: Fortress Press, 1972), 3–24; George Forell, *Faith Active in Love: An Investigation of the Principles Underlying Luther's Social Ethics* (New York: American, 1954), 70–111; Lindberg, *Beyond Charity*, 91–100; Bernhard Lohse, *Martin Luther: An Introduction to His Life and Work*, trans. Robert Schultz (Philadelphia: Fortress Press, 1986), 129–30; Donald Ziemke, *Love for the Neighbor in Luther's Theology* (Minneapolis: Augsburg, 1963), 14–42.

37. In 1545 Luther wrote the preface to the complete edition of his Latin writings. The preface is an oft-quoted source of Luther's understanding of his theological awakening, albeit written in hindsight. In the preface he speaks of his spiritual turmoil and the theological breakthrough he experienced while studying the Letter of Paul to the Romans. "Though I lived as a monk without reproach, I felt that I was a sinner before God with an extremely disturbed conscience. I could not believe that he was placated by my satisfaction. I did not love, yes, I hated the righteous God who punishes sinners, and secretly, if not blasphemously, certainly murmuring greatly, I was angry with God, and said, 'As if, indeed, it is not enough, that miserable sinners, eternally lost through original sin, are crushed by every kind of calamity by the law of the Decalogue, without having God add pain to pain by the gospel and also by the gospel threatening us with his righteousness

and wrath!' Thus I raged with a fierce and troubled conscience. Nevertheless, I beat importunately upon Paul at that place, most ardently desiring to know what St. Paul wanted. At last, by the mercy of God, meditating day and night, I gave heed to the context of the words, namely, 'In it the righteousness of God is revealed, as it is written, "He who through faith is righteous shall live."' There I began to understand that the righteousness of God is that by which the righteous lives by a gift of God, namely, by faith. And this is the meaning: the righteousness of God is revealed by the gospel, namely, the passive righteousness with which merciful God justifies us by faith, as it is written, 'He who through faith is righteous shall live.' Here I felt that I was altogether born again and had entered paradise itself through open gates." *LW* 34:336-337.

38. Ibid.

39. By the sixteenth century entrance into religious life as a hermit, monk, nun, friar, or sister was promoted and perceived as a superior Christian calling, not simply a different way to live one's life as a Christian. Thus, the distinction emerged between "religious" clergy and "secular" (that is, diocesan) clergy. The latter were physically and symbolically "closer" to lay Christians and the "temptations" that faced people who lived in "the world." In the "trickle down" theory of the late medieval spiritual economy, many believed that one would have a greater chance of growing in "holiness" if one were a member of a religious order, seemingly "removed" from the "temptations of the world." By the early sixteenth century, however, numerous satirical songs and cartoons that mocked the economic and social privileges of the monastic and mendicant orders were also prominent. For commentary and cartoons, see A. G. Dickens, *Reformation and Society in Sixteenth-Century Europe* (New York: Harcourt, Brace & World, 1966), 29-51; Heiko Oberman, *Luther: Man between God and the Devil*, trans. Eileen Walliser-Schwarzbart (New York: Image Doubleday, 1992), 50–81; Scribner, *For the Sake of Simple Folk*, 37–59, 95–147.

40. Luther's *existential* concern refers to his own sense of anxiety. The remaining terms refer to the different categories that would constitute the study of Christianity: for example, *theological,* Christian understandings of God; *hermeneutical,* the method one uses in the interpretation of the Bible; *soteriological,* the theology of salvation;

sacramental, the theology and study of the origins, number, celebration, and effects of the sacraments; *ecclesial,* the theology of the church.

4. A Peasant Becomes a Priest

1. *LW* 44:118–19.

2. The bull condemned forty-one claims attributed to Luther, demanded that all copies of his works be destroyed, and prohibited any preaching, teaching, publishing, printing, translating, praising, or defending of his writings. See Leo X, *Bulla contra errores Martini Lutheri et sequatium* (Landschut: Johann Weissenberger, 1521).

3. See R. W. Scribner, *For the Sake of Simple Folk,* 20–21, on Haug Marschalck who interpreted Luther as a prophetic figure in his 1523 acronym: *L* = *Lautere* (proclaimer) of evangelical truth; *U* = *Uberflussige gnad* (overflowing grace) of the Holy Spirit; *T* = *Trewlich diener* (loyal servant) of Christ; *H* = *Helian* (Elias) and *E* = *Enoch* who exposed the Antichrist; *R* = *Rabi* (Rabbi), for he has mastered all defilers of Scripture. It was the artist Hans Holbein the Younger who portrayed Luther as Hercules.

4. *LW* 44:118. Luther's comments on Roman avarice were written in "The Papacy at Rome, an Answer to the Celebrated Romanist at Leipzig," in reference to a work by one of Luther's opponents, the Franciscan friar Augustine von Alveld.

5. "To the Christian Nobility of the German Nation Concerning the Reform of the Christian Estate," *LW* 44:123–217

6. *LW* 44:127.

7. Ibid.

8. Ibid.

9. *LW* 44:130. I recognize that Luther's argument concerning the "spiritual" and "secular" estates would lead him to claim that the work of Christian rulers (the "temporal" power) must be extended to "punish and use force whenever guilt deserves or necessity demands, without regard to whether the culprit is pope, bishop, or priest" (*LW* 44:131). The first critique was aimed at securing a theological foundation for the reform of the church by Christians, whether priest (as in Luther's case) or ruler (as in the case of Frederick, the elector of Saxony). By rejecting the medieval idea that the spiritual estate was superior to the secular estate, Luther intended to strip the former of any canonical

immunities that would prevent the movement of reform from proceeding. At the same time, however, I focus here on his teaching concerning the "universal priesthood of the baptized" because that teaching would have long-reaching effects in the promotion of social reform.

10. "The pope or bishop anoints, shaves heads, ordains, consecrates, and prescribes garb different from that of the laity, but he can never make a [person] into a Christian or into a spiritual [person] by so doing. He might well make a [person] into a hypocrite or a humbug and blockhead, but never a Christian." *LW* 44:127.

11. *LW* 44:129.

12. Ibid. Luther does not make the leap from baptismal consecration, available for all, to the community's selection of women for public ministry. In this regard he accepted much of the biology, gender roles, and theology of his time. While he agreed with the inherited interpretation of Genesis 2–3 that placed women in a subordinate position to men (although he insisted that the lopsided dynamic could never serve as grounds for boasting or abuse by men), he seemed at times to hold forth the tantalizing idea that in baptism this subordination was reversed not only spiritually but also socially.

13. *LW* 44:128.

14. This was not an unknown practice in medieval Christianity: Benedictine monastic communities elected abbots, usually for lifelong terms; the Dominicans elected all their leaders (superiors) for terms of office after which the official (the local prior, the regional provincial, or the master of the order) would return to other work in the community as a brother (*frater*).

15. I say, "*shifted attention* from episcopal leadership." Luther did not seek to eliminate the ordained ministry nor supervision of regions by a pastor elected as supervisor or bishop. The former was necessary for the proclamation of the gospel and the celebration of the sacraments of the gospel. One could argue that the ordained ministry participated in the *esse* (essence) of the church, whereas supervisors or bishops supported the *bene esse* (well-being, welfare) of the church. At any rate the reality of leadership in the church, Luther insisted, was judged by and at the service of the proclamation of the gospel in word and sacrament in accord with the central Lutheran axiom: justification by grace through faith.

16. *LW* 44:128; emphasis mine.

17. *LW* 44:134.

18. *LW* 44:135.

19. *LW* 44:133–36.

20. Peter Matheson, *The Imaginative World of the Reformation* (Minneapolis: Fortress Press, 2001), 9.

21. *LW* 44:128.

22. *LW* 44:130.

23. *LW* 12:312.

24. *The Book of Concord: The Confessions of the Evangelical Lutheran Church* [hereafter *BC*], ed. Robert Kolb and Timothy J. Wengert; trans. Charles Arand, Eric Gritsch, Robert Kolb, William Russell, James Schaaf, Jane Strohl, Timothy J. Wengert (Minneaplis: Fortress Press, 2000), 432–33.

25. *LW* 14:114.

26. *BC* 433.

27. *LW* 24:67.

28. *LW* 1:15.

29. *LW* 45:331.

30. *LW* 2:29.

31. *LW* 4:5.

32. *LW* 7:184.

5. *Consider the Broad Fields*

1. "We must . . . sweep out this filth of the devil and throw it away; we must cleanse this doctrine well and impress it on the hearts of men. One must teach and believe: 'I must and will hear or see no work, no worship of God, no spirituality, no holy life other than that of this man Christ, or that which he transmitted to the apostles, and the apostles, in turn, transmitted to the preachers. When I hear these, I hear Christ Himself; and when I hear Christ, I hear the Father.' Thus all must be woven together and interrelated. And if the relationship is right, all must follow in a straight line. It is like tracing and following a river or a brook to its source, the spring. I drink the water from the pipes. It comes from the brooklet; and this, in the end, flows from the spring." *LW* 24:70, 71.

2. *D. Martin Luthers Werke: Kritische Gesamtausgabe, Briefwechsel* (Weimar: Hermann Böhlaus Nachfolger, 1930), 1.74, 33.

3. See "Justification," 25–42.

4. *LW* 35:118.

5. *LW* 35:119.

6. Ibid.

7. *LW* 35:120.

8. See Dietmar Lage, *Martin Luther's Christology and Ethics* (Lewiston: Mellen, 1990), 93–105, on Luther's use of *sacramentum* and *exemplum* in his "christological ethics"; and Donald Ziemke, *Love for the Neighbor in Luther's Theology* (Minneapolis: Augsburg, 1963), 51–64, on the role of the same distinction in Luther's social ethics.

9. *LW* 35:121.

10. *LW* 35:123.

11. Eberhard Schendel, "Martin Luther und die Armen," *Lutherischen Kirche in der Welt* 36 (1989): 113–14.

12. See Henri de Lubac, *Exégèse médiévale: Les quatre sens de l'Écriture* (Paris: Aubier, 1959), and Beryl Smalley, *The Study of the Bible in the Middle Ages* (New York: Philosophical Library, 1952).

13. "You will not find a single letter in the whole Bible that agrees with what you, along with Origen and Jerome, call the 'spiritual meaning.' St. Paul calls it *mysteria*, that is, veiled and secret meaning. Therefore, the earliest fathers called it *anagogas*, that is, 'the more withdrawn meanings, separate knowledge' (*remotiores sensus, separatas intelligentias*). At times they also called it 'allegory,' as St. Paul himself does, Galatians 4[:24]; but this is not yet Spirit, although the Spirit grants this as well as the letter and all gifts. As we read in 1 Corinthians 14[:2], 'The Spirit utters the hidden meaning.' Some people, out of ignorance, therefore, attributed a fourfold meaning to Scripture: the literal, the allegorical, the anagogical, and the tropological. But there is no basis for it." *LW* 39:180. Luther noted his seeming abandonment of the fourfold sense of Scripture in his ongoing debate with Jerome Esmer of the University of Leipzig. Luther clarified his understanding of the "letter" and the "spirit" of Scripture and indicated why he sought the literal sense, when best, and the spiritual sense when appropriate. His criticism of Esmer continued into a charge brought against Rome: they had transformed "Spirit" (which brings life, grace, and freedom to the

Christian) into the letter of the law (which brings only mandates, judgment, and death).

14. *LW* 35:122; see also *LW* 10:3-5 where Luther offers a schema of the fourfold sense of Scripture as prelude to his lectures on the Psalms.

15. *D. Martin Luthers Werke, Kritisch Gesamtausgabe* (Weimar: Hermann Böhlaus Nachfolger, 1885), 1.52, 15–18.

16. *LW* 11:38.

17. There is a long tradition that refers to this as a "prophetic" interpretation of the Hebrew Bible, finding the "New" in the "Old" Testament, that is, finding figures or events narrated in the New Testament "prophetically" mentioned in the Hebrew Bible. It remains a popular approach among many Christians, one that continues to cultivate the notion that the Hebrew Bible serves largely or only as a prelude to the Christian New Testament, thus robbing the Hebrew Scriptures of their own integrity. Such a viewpoint tends to blur the distinction between the Christian use of Hebrew Bible images or sayings to *understand* the figure of Jesus and other Christian realities and the notion, alive in most of Christian history, that the Hebrew Bible is largely a *prediction* of the birth, life, and death of Jesus of Nazareth. See Gail Ramshaw's discussion of the Christian use of the Hebrew Scriptures, part of her magisterial work on images in the Bible and Christian lectionaries, in *Treasures Old and New: Images in the Lectionary* (Minneapolis: Fortress Press, 2002), 9–50.

18. Ps. 22:1.

19. Paul W. Robinson, "Luther's Explanation of *Daily Bread* in Light of Medieval Preaching," *Lutheran Quarterly* 13 (Winter 1999): 435–47. Robinson notes that Luther's interpretation of "daily bread" changes over the course of his career, the spiritual sense supplemented by the plain or literal sense. This shift in interpretation, he argues, appears by 1528 in the first catechetical sermon of that year.

20. Peter Matheson, *The Imaginative World of the Reformation* (Minneapolis: Fortress Press, 2001), 42–43.

21. Genesis 40–45, Joseph's preparation for and supervision of a "national" food distribution system during a time of famine. See *LW* 7:156–97, 203–6, 213–15; 8:3–72.

22. *LW* 35:123.

23. *LW* 2:17.

24. *LW* 31:345.

25. *LW* 23:9-10. Here Luther is commenting on the words of Jesus in John 6. In "the Babylonian Captivity of the Church," he argued that this text from John refers not to the sacrament but to faith in the incarnate Word. See *LW* 36:19.

26. *LW* 21:347.

27. *LW* 53:233: *"Es wolle Gott Uns Gnädig sein."* The St. Louis Edition reads, "Thy word it is both bed and board and for all folk availeth." The translation quoted here is by Richard Massie, *Lutheran Book of Worship* (Minneapolis and Philadelphia: Augsburg Publishing House and Board of Publication, Lutheran Church in America, 1978), 335.

28. *LW* 36:35.

29. *LW* 23:11.

30. *LW* 35:54.

31. From the Greek *askesis* ("exercise" or "training"), the practice of an "ascetic" life was not uniquely Christian but known by the Stoics and Cynics as well as the writers of Hebrew wisdom literature. Early advocates of Christian asceticism drew inspiration from the words of Jesus, "If any want to become my followers, let them deny themselves and take up their cross and follow me" (Mark 8:34), and Paul, "Athletes exercise self-control in all things; they do it to receive a perishable wreath, but we an imperishable one" (1 Cor. 9:25). The wide diversity found in early Christian asceticism was gradually focused by the late medieval period, albeit not exclusively, with monastic and mendicant orders. Lay ascetic movements did emerge throughout the high and late Middle Ages, in part as protests against the corruption of the clergy and the wealth amassed by religious communities; in part, as the search for a simple way to imitate the "poor, property-less, and wandering Christ" (e.g., the Waldensians and the Beguines).

32. *LW* 11:316–43, especially his commentary on verses 11, 13–15, and 27.

33. *LW* 11:342.

34. Matheson, *Imaginative World of the Reformation*, 43.

35. The tendency to see the realities of this earth, "matter," as shadows of or subordinate to "heavenly" realities, "spirit." If the medieval world was focused on the pilgrimage from this earthly life

to a "heavenly" life, it is not surprising to see the convergence of a Christianized Neoplatonism in the monastic framework that so decisively shaped medieval Christianity for close to seven hundred years. See Jean Leclercq, *The Love of Learning and the Desire for God: A Study of Monastic Culture*, trans. Catherine Misrahi (New York: Fordham University Press, 1961).

36. Robinson, "Luther's Explanation of *Daily Bread*," 442, in reference to Albrecht Peters, *Kommentar zu Luthers Katechismen* (Göttingen: Vandenhoeck & Ruprecht, 1990), 3:117–18.

37. Johannes Schwanke, "Luther on Creation," in *Harvesting Martin Luther's Reflections on Theology, Ethics, and the Church*, ed. Timothy Wengert, *Lutheran Quarterly Books* (Grand Rapids: Eerdmans, 2004), 92. Schwanke emphasizes the lectures on Genesis (1535–45) in his study of Luther's theology of creation.

38. The Large Catechism, in *BC* 432–33.

39. Ibid., 449–52.

40. Ibid., 451.

41. The Small Catechism, in *BC* 354.

42. The Large Catechism, in *BC* 432.

43. *LW* 2:76.

44. Ibid.

45. Luther's teaching on the ubiquity of Christ, the Word of God, throughout the creation emerged in his debate with Zwingli and others concerning Christ's presence in the Lord's Supper. See, among other writings, his "That These Words of Christ, 'This Is My Body,' Still Stand Firm against the Fanatics" (*LW* 37:13–150) with commentary by H. Paul Santmire, *The Travail of Nature: The Ambiguous Ecological Promise of Christian Theology* (Minneapolis: Fortress Press, 1985), 121–33; idem, "So That He Might Fill All Things: Comprehending the Cosmic Love of Christ," *Dialog* 42, no. 3 (September 2003): 257–78, in particular 266–69; Frank Senn, *Christian Liturgy: Catholic and Evangelical* (Minneapolis: Fortress Press, 1997), 307–10.

46. Schwanke, "Luther on Creation," 82.

47. *LW* 2:75.

48. Justo Gonzáles, *Christian Thought Revisited: Three Types of Theology*, rev. ed. (Maryknoll: Orbis, 1999), 25. In this highly engaging study of three forms of early Christian thought influenced by Jewish,

Hellenistic, and Latin cultures and their subsequent influence in Western theology and practice, Gonzáles provides a helpful link between what he calls "Type C theology," represented by Irenaeus of Lyons (what I consider a theology shaped by Jewish sensibilities), and Luther. See 107–21.

49. *LW* 1:72.

50. *LW* 1:205–14. While Luther discusses the labor needed to produce food, he also comments on German farm production and the failure of the mendicant orders to work for their food, an indictment of institutionalized and church-approved begging.

51. *LW* 5:9-10.

52. Throughout his Genesis commentary, Luther notes the testing of the righteous and the punishment of the unrighteous through natural disaster. "All the godly at all times have endured famine and the slanders of the godless; and the saintlier they were, the more punishments and disasters there were in the world, not that they themselves caused them and disturbed the world, but because the world spurned the light of the Word and engaged in idolatry," *LW* 5:10. Here Luther reflects the prescientific worldview in which the books of the Bible were written: supernatural forces cause natural disasters.

53. *LW* 51:177.

54. *LW* 51:161.

55. "Treatise on Good Works" (1520); "Ten Sermons on the Catechism" (1528); "The Large Catechism" (1529).

56. See Ricardo W. Reith, "Luther on Greed," *Lutheran Quarterly* 15 (2001): 336–51, in which the author highlights Luther's use and interpretation of Ephesians 5:5 ("The one who is greedy is an idolater"). "[Luther] affirmed that this passage forbids to Christians all forms of spoliation against their neighbor and all quarrels over material things" (338).

57. Ibid., 337.

58. *LW* 44:109.

59. *LW* 4:381.

60. Ibid.

61. *LW* 4:382.

62. *LW* 51:8.

63. *LW* 44:109.

64. For Luther wherever the Word of God is bringing faith in the promises of God to life, there is the church. Thus, he speaks about various figures in the Old Testament who manifested trust in the Word of God as participants in the "church."

65. *LW* 3:180.

66. *LW* 3:178.

67. *LW* 3:180.

68. *LW* 3:181. "Today in Germany many pastors of churches almost starve. Poor Christ is hungry. Everywhere He all but perishes from His afflictions. Indeed, there is no compassion among human beings." *LW* 3:249.

69. *LW* 3:184.

70. *LW* 3:183–84.

71. *LW* 3:184.

72. *LW* 3:183.

73. *LW* 7:135.

74. *LW* 7:161–62.

75. *LW* 7:159.

76. *LW* 7:219.

77. Ibid.

78. *LW* 44:108.

79. *LW* 1:68-73, 101–19, 203–19.

80. *LW* 2:75-80.

81. *LW* 3:176–99.

82. *LW* 7:148–61.

83. *LW* 9:92–98.

84. *LW* 4:137.

85. *LW* 13:400–401.

86. *LW* 18:161–62.

87. *LW* 17:286–87.

88. Large Catechism, 452.

89. *LW* 45:286.

90. *LW* 52:11. While claiming and emphasizing the humanity of Christ (in which the glory of God and Christ's own divinity are "hidden"), Luther nonetheless affirms his "sinlessness."

91. *LW* 12:115.

92. *LW* 3:50.

93. Large Cathechism, 449–50.

94. Luther's "Sermons on the Catechism" were preached in 1528 just before the publication of the Large Catechism. In this excerpt he comments on the fourth petition: "'Give us this day our daily bread.' This is beginning to be understood, though there are few who do understand it. When you pray this petition, turn your eyes to every- thing that can prevent our bread from coming and the crops from prospering. Therefore extend your thoughts to all the fields and do not see only the baker's oven. You pray, therefore, against the devil and the world, who can hinder the grain by tempest and war. We pray also for temporal peace against war because in times of war we cannot have bread. Likewise, you pray for government, for sustenance and peace, without which you cannot eat: Grant, Lord, that the grain may prosper, that the princes may keep the peace, that war may not break out, that we may give thanks to thee in peace. Therefore it would be proper to stamp the emperor's or the princes' coat-of-arms upon bread as well as upon money or coins. Few know that this is included in the Lord's Prayer. Though the Lord gives bread in sufficient abundance even to the wicked and godless, it is nevertheless fitting that we Chris- tians should know and acknowledge that it comes from God, that we realize that bread, hunger, and war are in God's hands. If he opens his hand, we have bread and all things in abundance; if he closes it then it is the opposite. Therefore, do not think that peace is an accidental thing; it is the gift of God.

"This petition, therefore, is directed against everything that hin- ders bread, including also base coinage . . . he who hinders bread and injures the people, let him be afraid of this petition. Thus it is a peti- tion against tempest, war, false buyers and sellers; against all of these this prayer cries out. Do not be afraid of the rich people; Duke Hans gets enough to eat from them; but fear the groans and tears of those who pray: 'Give us this day our daily bread,' i.e., defend us from fam- ine and evil men, that they may not deprive us of bread.

"Bread cannot come to me if there is no peace, so that there are just prices in the market, so that there is no bloodshed. Defend us from skinners and usurers! [The explanation of] 'daily' and 'this day' belongs in the sharp sermons. The Lord does indeed give bread, but he also wants us to pray, in order that we acknowledge it as his gift. This again is a great need, which pertains to the body." *LW* 51:176.

95. Robinson, "Luther's Explanation of *Daily Bread*," 443–44.

96. *LW* 3:184.

97. *LW* 9:147.

98. *LW* 26:105–6.

99. *LW* 44:71.

100. Ibid.

101. *LW* 3:182.

102. *LW* 3:187.

103. *LW* 44:85–86.

104. Large Catechism, 409.

105. Ibid.

106. *LW* 7:158–59.

107. *LW* 7:159.

108. Large Catechism, 450–51. In his commentary on Psalm 82 (*LW* 13:42–72), Luther set forth the duties of the prince. At once he speaks admirably, even idealistically, of the good a prince can do for his people. Yet he also speaks in a realistic manner, touched with a hint of despair, about the failures of princes in his own day to care for the needs of their people.

109. *LW* 3:244.

6. Holding All Things in Common

1. Theodore Bachmann, introduction to "The Blessed Sacrament of the Holy and True Body of Christ, and the Brotherhoods" (1519), *LW* 35:48.

2. *LW* 35:49. Here Luther suggests that both wine and bread form the sacramental sign. While he is aware of the late medieval practice in which bread alone was given to the laity while priests received both elements, he nonetheless suggests that both bread and wine be given to the laity.

3. *LW* 35:50.

4. *LW* 35:51.

5. Latin *com-munus*, hence *communere*, whence comes English *communion*, refers to a sharing of gifts, services, duties, or functions. Latin *munus* also serves as the root of *municipality*, an urban political reality.

6. *LW* 35:51.

7. *LW* 35:51–52.

8. *LW* 35:53.

9. *LW* 35:54.

10. *LW* 35:61-62.

11. *LW* 35:61.

12. *LW* 35:67.

13. *LW* 35:69.

14. *The Europe of the Devout: The Catholic Reformation and the Formation of a New Society* (Cambridge: Cambridge University Press, 1989), 133.

15. *LW* 35:69.

16. *LW* 35:56–57.

17. *LW* 35:57.

18. *LW* 45:172–73.

19. *LW* 35:68.

20. See Martha Stortz, "Practicing What It Means: Welfare Reform and the Lord's Supper," in *Currents in Theology and Mission* 26, no. 1 (February 1999): 30.

21. "The Babylonian Captivity of the Church" (1520), *LW* 36:37. See Gordon Lathrop, "The Christian Sacrifice," in his *Holy Things: A Liturgical Theology* (Minneapolis: Fortress Press, 1993), 139–58; Frank Senn, "Luther's Liturgical Reforms," in his *Christian Liturgy: Catholic and Evangelical* (Minneapolis: Fortress, 1999), 267–75; and Gordon Lathrop, "A Contemporary Lutheran Approach to Worship and Culture: Sorting Out the Principles," in *Worship and Culture in Dialogue*, ed. S. Anita Stauffer (Geneva: Lutheran World Federation, 1994), 137–51.

22. *LW* 4:381.

23. On worship: Lathrop, "Contemporary Lutheran Approach to Worship and Culture," 137–51; on ethics: Paul Althaus, *The Ethics of Martin Luther*, trans. Robert Schultz (Philadelphia: Fortress Press, 1972), 3–24. For Luther the teaching on justification by grace is the central teaching of Scripture; it is a biblical principle. That all Scripture points to Christ is, for Luther, a claim derived from his study of the Bible but one that was also influenced by his familiarity with the *devotio moderna* and its Christocentric spirituality. At the same time "Lutheran" theology so fully incorporated the teaching on justification

by grace that one can also speak of this biblical "center" as a theological conviction or principle.

24. Carter Lindberg, *Beyond Charity*, 100.

25. *LW* 36:18.

26. *LW* 36:21. "The sacrament does not belong to the priests, but to all men. The priests are not lords, but servants in duty bound to administer both kinds to those who desire them, as often as they desire them" (27).

27. *LW* 36:32.

28. Ibid.

29. *LW* 36:35.

30. *LW* 36:35–36.

31. *LW* 36:36: "Now as they were eating, Jesus took bread, and blessed, and broke it, and gave it to his disciples and said, 'Take, eat; this is my body, which is given for you.' And he took a cup, and when he had given thanks he gave it to them, saying, 'Drink of it, all of you; for this cup is the new testament in my blood, which is poured out for you and for many for the forgiveness of sins. Do this in remembrance of me.' " Four texts have been harmonized by Luther: Matt. 26:26-28; Mark 14:22-24; Luke 22:19-20; 1 Cor. 11:23-25.

32. *LW* 36:37.

33. *LW* 36:38.

34. *LW* 36:40.

35. *LW* 36:39.

36. See *LW* 36:51-56, in which Luther offers reforms concerning liturgical language, ritual practice at the altar, and devotional practices related to the Mass.

37. *LW* 36:53

38. *LW* 12:104.

39. In *Beyond Charity*, 200–202, Lindberg has provided an English translation of the Wittenberg 1522 Order found in *Die evangelischen Kirchenordnung des 16. Jahrhundert*, ed., Emil Sehling (Tübingen: Mohr, 1902), 1:697–98. In his "Address to the Christian Nobility of the German Nation" of 1520 (*LW* 44:189), Luther argued that each city, rather than monastery or cathedral clergy, should care for its poor: "Nobody ought to go begging among Christians. It would even be a very simple matter to make a law to the effect that every city should look after its

own poor, if only we had the courage and the intention to do so."

40. See *LW* 45:161–68 for the history of the parish, speculation regarding the written correspondence and visits between Luther and town representatives, and the publication date of the preface and ordinance.

41. *LW* 45:172–73. In the preface Luther notes that while monastic property may be seized by evangelical governing authorities, the resident monks or friars are not to be expelled and treated harshly, especially if they are elderly or have no trade. They are to be supported until they die since there can be no force in receiving the gospel: "Matters are to be determined by Christian love and not by strict human justice" (172).

42. *LW* 45:176.

43. *LW* 45:177.

44. *LW* 45:179–81.

45. *LW* 45:177.

46. With the exception of the Jewish population in Germany, Luther imagined a society in which church and state were distinguished yet coextensive: to be German was to be Christian. City councils that received the Lutheran reform were city councils made up of "evangelicals" or "Lutherans." While pastors did not usually serve as mayors, they were also citizens of the city and participants in the deliberations of the town or city councils. Although he would carefully distinguish the duties of pastors who preach the gospel in service to the reign of Christ from the duties of civic rulers who make and enforce laws "to discourage the wicked and protect the innocent," and insist that the two should never be confused, he nonetheless recognized that theology and faith could and should inform and shape the social commitments of Christians.

47. *LW* 45:192.

48. For Lutheran and other Protestant social welfare initiatives, see Miriam Usher Chrisman, "Urban Poor in the Sixteenth Century: The Case of Strasbourg," in Miriam Usher Chrisman and Otto Gründler, eds., *Social Groups and Religious Ideas in the Sixteenth Century* (Kalamazoo: Medieval Institute, 1978), 59–67; Ole Peter Grell and Andrew Cunningham, "The Reformation and Changes in Welfare Provision in Early Modern Northern Europe," *Health Care and Poor Relief in Protestant Europe, 1500–1700*, ed. Ole Grell and Andrew Cunningham

(London: Routledge, 1997), 1–42; Carter Lindberg, " 'There Should Be No Beggars among Christians': Karlstadt, Luther, and the Origins of Protestant Poor Relief," *Church History* 46 (1977): 313–34; Charles Parker, "Calvinism and Poor Relief in Reformation Holland," *The Reformation of Charity: The Secular and the Religious in Early Modern Poor Relief*, ed. Thomas Max Safely (Boston: Brill, 2003), 107–20; Mary Sprunger, "Mennonites and Sectarian Poor Relief in Golden-Age Amsterdam," *The Reformation of Charity*, 137–53; Lee Palmer Wandel, *Always among Us: Images of the Poor in Zwingli's Zurich* (Cambridge: Cambridge University Press, 1990); William Wright, "A Closer Look at House Poor Relief through the Common Chest and Indigence in Sixteenth-Century Hesse," *Archiv für Reformationsgeschichte* 70 (1979): 225–38.

49. See the comprehensive work by Michel Mollat, *The Poor in the Middle Ages*, trans. Arthur Goldhammer (New Haven: Yale University Press, 1987), especially 191–294 on late medieval and early modern perceptions of the poor. Lindberg, *Beyond Charity*, 18–33, offers a helpful summary of the early Christian and medieval Christian valorization of poverty.

50. *LW* 45:176.

51. *LW* 45:179.

52. *LW* 53:13.

53. *LW* 35:54.

7. Greed Is an Unbelieving Scoundrel

1. Alister McGrath, *Reformation Thought: An Introduction* (Oxford: Blackwell, 1999), 5–11.

2. See Samuel Torvend, "The Whole Bible Painted in Our Houses: Visual Narrative and Religious Polemic in Early Lutheran Art," *Institute of Liturgical Studies: Occasional Papers* 11, ed. Rhoda Schuler (Valparaiso: Institute of Liturgical Studies, 2006), 45–62.

3. *LW* 31:52-53.

4. "Greed was normally seen as a negative quality or a bad behavior, irrational and unjust, as sin and addiction. Such was the predominant opinion at Luther's time." Ricardo W. Reith, "Luther on Greed," *Lutheran Quarterly* 15 (2001): 153. See also 154–155 on unbelief as the root of injustice.

5. *LW* 31:300.

6. *LW* 31:293–306.

7. *LW* 31:300.

8. *LW* 44:115–217.

9. *LW* 36:3–126.

10. *LW* 31:327–77.

11. "A Brief Instruction on What to Look for and Expect in the Gospels," *LW* 35:113–24.

12. "Brief Sermon on Usury" (1519) and "Long Sermon on Usury" (1520) were combined, expanded, and then published as "Trade and Usury" (1520). See *LW* 45:233–310.

13. *LW* 45:239.

14. *LW* 13:52–54.

15. Reith, "Luther on Greed," 168.

16. "The merchants have a common rule which is their chief maxim and the basis of all their sharp practices, when they say: I may sell my goods as dear as I can. They think this is their right. Thus, occasion is given to avarice, and every window and door to hell is opened. What else does it mean but this: I care nothing about my neighbor; so long as I have my profit and satisfy my greed, of what concern is it to me if it injures my neighbor in ten ways at once." *LW* 45:247.

17. *LW* 45:270.

18. *LW* 45:262.

19. *LW* 45:263–64.

20. *LW* 45:272.

21. *LW* 2:263.

22. *LW* 45:287.

23. Carter Lindberg, *Beyond Charity*, 97.

24. Ibid.

25. *LW* 35:48.

26. "It is not now nor ever has been our intention to abolish the liturgical service of God completely, but rather to purify the one that is now in use from the wretched accretions which corrupt it and to point out an evangelical use." *LW* 53:19.

27. *LW* 35:67.

28. *LW* 35:61.

29. *LW* 35:54.

30. *LW* 35:57.

31. My paraphrase of Cynthia Moe-Lobeda's assertion in her "Globalization in Light of Luther's Eucharistic Economic Ethics," *Dialog: A Journal of Theology* 42, no. 3 (Fall 2003): 252.

32. *LW* 35:61.

33. *BC* 68.

34. *LW* 35:61.

35. On the application of justification by grace to sacramental reform and the "breaking of symbols," here the symbolic activity of the Mass, to a wider need beyond the Christian assembly, see Gordon Lathrop, *Holy People: A Liturgical Ecclesiology* (Minneapolis: Fortress Press, 1999), 161–63, 183–201.

36. *BC* 356.

37. *BC* 347.

38. James Kittleson, *Luther the Reformer* (Minneapolis: Augsburg, 1986), 217.

39. *LW* 35:57.

40. *LW* 45:245–46.

41. *LW* 45:241.

42. *LW* 45:272.

43. Reported in Luther's letter of November 24, 1524, to Spalatin. See *LW* 45:166–67, n. 32.

44. *LW* 41:149.

45. *LW* 44:127–31. That baptism initiates the Christian into priestly service in the world is also noted in "Two Kinds of Righteousness" (1519), "The Blessed Sacrament of the Holy and True Body of Christ, and the Brotherhoods" (1519), "The Babylonian Captivity of the Church" (1520), "The Freedom of a Christian" (1520), and "A Brief Instruction on What to Look for and Expect in the Gospels" (1522).

46. *LW* 31:358.

47. *LW* 31:365.

48. *LW* 45:170.

49. *LW* 45:189.

INDEX OF SCRIPTURE

INDEX OF SUBJECTS AND NAMES

116–17; and baptism, 45–49; and creation, 70, 73; and ethics, 147n36; and feeding the hungry, 85–86, 133–34; and reform of the Mass, 102–3, 123, 165 n 35; and Scripture. 62–65, 160n23; and social welfare, 98–99

Karlstadt, Andreas, 163n48
Keys of the kingdom. *See* Forgiveness
Kind, Heinrich, 125
Kittleson, James, 130

Labor, 54, 80–81, 110–11, 118, 121, 133, 156n50
Lage, Dietmar, 152n8
Laity, 22, 45–46, 48–50, 52, 54–55, 101, 105–10, 124–30
The Large Catechism, x, 70, 71, 81–83, 87–88, 158n94
Lathrop, Gordon, xii, 138n9, 146n28, 160n21,n23, 165n35
Laziness, 77, 80
Leipzig, University of, 152n13
Leisnig Ordinance, 105–13, 119–20, 122–23, 124–25, 132–33. *See also Preface to the Ordinance of a Common Chest*
Leo X, 19, 43, 92, 149n2
Liberation theology, 145n12
Lindberg, Carter, xii, 35, 122, 140n2, 141 n, 14, 143n25,n29, 146n21, 147n36, 161n24,n39, 163n48,n49, 164n23
Lis, Catharina and Hugo Soly, 17, 141n14
Little, Lester, 143n29

Liturgy, 97–98, 123–25
Loans, 106, 110, 121–22
Lombard, Peter, 45
Lord's Supper. *See* Mass
Lortz, Joseph, 21
Love, Christ's, 29–30, 63, 65, 95, 97, 107; for one's neighbor, 33, 36, 64–65, 67, 75–76, 86, 94, 97–99, 98–99, 102, 107, 119, 125, 142n22; for the needy, 106, 107, 108, 109, 134; God's, 29, 51, 63; and the sacrament, 94–95, 113, 125–26
Love feasts. *See* Agape meal
Louvain, University of, 43
Luder, Hans, 41
Luther, Martin, as critique of unjust economic practices, 76–77, 82–83, 95–97, 120–23, 128–33; as interpreter of the Bible, 59–70; as monastic priest and scholar, 13–19; as public reformer, 43–45; as reformer of baptism, 45–55, and the Mass, 91–105; as reformer of social welfare, 97–100, 105–13; as Wittenberg nightingale, 25–26

McGrath, Alister, 115, 163n1
Magdeburg, 18
Malnourishment, ix, 17–18
Margaret of Brunswick, 92
Masks of God, 51–55
Mass, the, as Christ coming to Christian community, 97; as Christ's new testament, 98–99, 102; as common possession of all Christians, 93–94; as commodity, 21–22, 68, 92,